IT'S NEVER TOO LATE

IT'S NEVER TOO LATE

by Ron Aldridge

JOSEF WEINBERGER PLAYS

LONDON

IT'S NEVER TOO LATE
First published in 2005
by Josef Weinberger Ltd
12-14 Mortimer Street, London, W1T 3JJ
www.josef-weinberger.com
general.info@jwmail.co.uk

Copyright © 2006 by Ron Aldridge
Copyright © 2005 by Ron Aldridge as an unpublished dramatic composition

The author asserts his moral right to be identified as the author of the work.

ISBN 0 85676 286 5

This play is protected by Copyright. According to Copyright Law, no public performance or reading of a protected play or part of that play may be given without prior authorisation from Josef Weinberger Plays, as agent for the Copyright Owners.

From time to time it is necessary to restrict or even withdraw the rights of certain plays. **It is therefore essential to check with us before making a commitment to produce a play.**

**NO PERFORMANCE MAY BE GIVEN WITHOUT A LICENCE**

AMATEUR PRODUCTIONS
Royalties are due at least one calendar month prior to the first performance. A royalty quotation will be issued upon receipt of the following details:

Name of Licensee
Play Title
Place of Performance
Dates and Number of Performances
Audience Capacity
Ticket Prices

PROFESSIONAL PRODUCTIONS
All enquiries regarding professional rights should be addressed to Josef Weinberger Plays at the above address. Enquiries for all other rights should be addressed to the author, c/o the publisher.

OVERSEAS PRODUCTIONS
Applications for productions overseas should be addressed to our local authorised agents. Further details are listed in our catalogue of plays, published every two years, or available from Josef Weinberger Plays at the address above.

CONDITIONS OF SALE
This book is sold subject to the condition that it shall not by way of trade or otherwise be resold, hired out, circulated or distributed without prior consent of the Publisher. **Reproduction of the text either in whole or part and by any means is strictly forbidden.**

Printed in England by Biddles Ltd, King's Lynn, Norfolk

IT'S NEVER TOO LATE was first presented by the Mill At Sonning Theatre (Sally Hughes, Artistic Director; David Vass, General Manager), on 22nd February 2005. The cast was as follows:

| | |
|---|---|
| SUSAN SHAW | Tina Gray |
| LINDA BRIDGES | Helen Cotterill |
| PETER BRIDGES | Nick Burnell |
| HENRY | Terrence Booth |
| THOMAS | Mark Bixter |
| RICHARD SHAW | Ron Aldridge |

Directed by Ron Aldridge
Set designed by Tony Eden
Costumes designed by Jane Kidd
Lighting designed by Matthew Biss
Choreography by Sarah Redmond

## CAST OF CHARACTERS

(in order of appearance)

Susan Shaw

Linda Bridges

Peter Bridges

Henry

Thomas

Richard Shaw

The action takes place in the living room of Susan Shaw's Victoran House. The Time is the present.

### ACT ONE

Scene One   A Thursday evening
Scene Two   A Thursday evening, one week later

### ACT TWO

Saturday, nine days later

## ACT ONE

## Scene One

*The setting is the living room of* SUSAN SHAW'S *Victorian house.*

*Upstage left is the front door of the house in a small hallway. The stairs lead from the hallway off stage right. Entrance to the main room is through a large alcove. Upstage right of the main room is a doorway leading to the kitchen. There is a bay window in the stage left wall, and french windows in the stage right wall. In the stage left area is a sofa and an armchair. In the stage right area is a table with five chairs around it. There is a sideboard along the upstage wall on which are some bottles of drink, glasses, the telephone, and a CD Player. The furniture and dressings, etc, are a tasteful blend of modern and antique.*

SUSAN *is upstage centre, by the sideboard, on the telephone.*

*Seated around the table, are* LINDA, PETER, HENRY *and* THOMAS, *all looking decidedly awkward and embarrassed.*

SUSAN (*on phone*) . . . oh really? . . . oh really? . . . oh really? . . . and how the hell could you possibly know what's best for me? . . . unreasonable! I'm being unreasonable? How dare you call me unreasonable in my own home on my own phone . . . oh really? . . . oh really? . . . well if you gave me a reason to be reasonable I'd have a reason to be reasonable . . . anyway, I don't wish to discuss it at the moment, I'm in the middle of a committee meeting . . . I said, I don't want to discuss it . . . burying my head in the sand? How dare you. I'd like to bury your head in something – preferably an industrial wine press . . . look, can't you stop thinking about yourself for one second and consider how I might be feeling . . . no you don't . . . no you don't, you have no idea . . . tell me then, come on, tell me how I'm feeling . . . oh no, don't want to do that do you? Well I'm going to tell you how I'm feeling right now whether you like it or not. I want you to think about the feeling you get when you suddenly discover you've just trodden in dog mess. Can you picture it?

(*We see the look of distaste on the faces of the others seated round the table.*)

Get the feeling?

(*The others all nod to each other.*)

That utter distaste? That is the feeling I get talking to you. And that is the thought I'd like to leave you with, because I have no wish to discuss the matter any further. Goodbye! (*She slams the phone down. She immediately picks it up again.*) And don't bother calling back! (*She slams the phone down again. She picks it up again.*) You're an arrogant little sod's-face and I don't know why I married you in the first place! (*She slams the phone down and storms off to the kitchen.*) The nerve of that man!

(*She has now gone. There is a moment as the others look at each other.*)

LINDA     I think she's just moved into the anger stage.

PETER     Oh really? And there's me thinking it was just idle banter.

LINDA     It's the next stage . . . it's progress, it's moving forward. This is not necessarily a bad thing.

HENRY     I don't like to see her so upset.

LINDA     Better this than how she's been for the past few weeks, believe me.

HENRY     Do you think she's coming back?

LINDA     She'll be back, Henry.

HENRY     Only we've still got one bit of business left before I'm able to conclude the meeting.

| | |
|---|---|
| LINDA | Just give her a minute or two. |
| HENRY | I don't want to conclude the meeting without her if she's . . . oh. |
| | (SUSAN *enters from the kitchen carrying a tray containing quiche, dips, etc, and some plates and cutlery. She crosses, and slams the tray onto the table. The others all slightly wince. She then storms back to the kitchen.*) |
| | Er, Susan, we've still got one bit of business . . . oh. |
| | (*She has gone.*) |
| PETER | I wonder what old Richard said to start this lot off? |
| LINDA | I don't know. But I like this anger. |
| HENRY | I'm finding it a little unnerving, I must say. And I would like to conclude this meeting . . . oh. |
| | (SUSAN *returns carrying two bottles of wine. She crosses, and slams these on the table. The others all wince again.*) |
| | Er, Susan . . . |
| SUSAN | Little sod! (*She turns and heads up to the sideboard.*) |
| HENRY | Oh. |
| LINDA | Not you, Henry. |
| | (*Alarming crashing noises then come from the cabinet as* SUSAN *collects some glasses.* LINDA *leaps up to help her.*) |
| LINDA | Here, let me help with those. |

*(They bring the glasses to the table.* PETER *starts to pour out the wine.)*

SUSAN  The nerve of that man. I tell you, I'm just so . . . angry!

PETER  Really? And there's me thinking it was just idle banter.

LINDA  Shut up, you. *(To* SUSAN.*)* So – the phone call was er . . .

SUSAN  Oh, wonderful. Just wonderful! *(She takes a large swig.)*

LINDA  Thought so. *(She takes a large swig, too.)*

SUSAN  Can you believe what he just said to me?

LINDA  Not until you tell me what he just said to you.

(SUSAN *looks at them.*)

SUSAN  He wants a divorce.

LINDA  A divorce? The little sod.

SUSAN  Can you believe it? He has an affair with a younger woman, leaves me and moves in with her, and now he wants a divorce. The nerve of the man. I'm the one that should be getting a divorce.

PETER  Why don't you, then?

SUSAN  Are you crazy? I'm not giving him a divorce.

LINDA  The little sod.

SUSAN  The little sod. "I want us to try and be friends" he said. "I want us to try and make it all right." Can you imagine? Be like trying to make a pig's ear out of a sow's arse.

| | |
|---|---|
| PETER | Er, I think you mean . . . |
| LINDA | Shut up, you, she knows what she means. |
| HENRY | I'm sorry to interrupt, but if I could just conclude . . . |
| SUSAN | I'm just so angry with him. |
| HENRY | I can see that, but there is one bit of business left. |
| LINDA | Well I think this anger of yours is good. It shows progress. |
| SUSAN | Doesn't feel like progress. |
| LINDA | But it is. You've had weeks of total despair, and this is the next stage. You keep this anger. |
| SUSAN | Not difficult, believe me. |
| HENRY | Er . . . this bit of business . . . |
| SUSAN | Oh how could he be so stupid? He can't possibly love this . . . this . . . Lisa. (*She spits.*) She could be his daughter. It's just ridiculous, a man of his age. And why? What's she got that I haven't? |
| PETER | Pert breasts? |
| LINDA | Peter! |
| PETER | She asked. |
| SUSAN | Oh, thank you very much. |
| LINDA | Excuse my moronic husband. Social graces are not his forte. |
| SUSAN | I'm quite proud of my breasts, if you must know. I think they've stood up quite well over the years. |

| | |
|---|---|
| PETER | What about the slim waist and the tight bum, then? |
| SUSAN | What about your paunch? |
| PETER | We're not talking about me. |
| LINDA | (*to* PETER) Will you stop! |
| SUSAN | Anyway, a good figure's not everything. I bet she can't cook. |
| PETER | Well they probably don't have much time for eating at the moment. |
| LINDA | Right, that's it. Go home now! |
| PETER | No, come on, come on, you know what it's like at the start. Can't keep your hands off each other. |
| LINDA | Will you stop being so insensitive. |
| PETER | I'm not being insensitive. I'm trying to help. |
| LINDA | Help? |
| PETER | I'm helping to maintain the anger. |
| LINDA | But it's not me that's supposed to be angry, you idiot. |
| PETER | Well calm down, then. What's the matter with you? |
| LINDA | What's the matter with me? What's the matter with you, you mean. Men. You're all the same. |
| PETER | What a ridiculous thing to say. Of course we're not all the same. I haven't run off with a younger woman yet. |
| LINDA | (*she stops*) What do you mean yet? |

| | |
|---|---|
| PETER | I didn't mean that. I didn't mean . . . |
| LINDA | Yes you did, you said yet. (*To others.*) He said "yet," didn't he? (*To* PETER.) You said "yet." What do you mean by "yet"? |
| PETER | I didn't mean to say . . . |
| LINDA | So who have you got your eye on, then? That one in the office is it? The one with the skirt the size of a hat band. Is that the one? |
| PETER | I haven't got my eye on anyone. |
| LINDA | We saw her the other day. She was wearing a jumper that was so tight she could hardly breathe. |
| PETER | That is not true. |
| THOMAS | (*loudly*) Excuse me. Excuse me! (*They all stop.*) Sorry. Sorry. But before we all get too carried away, perhaps we should conclude the meeting? |
| HENRY | Yes. Yes, good idea, Thomas. There's just one last bit of business. |
| SUSAN | All right, what is it? |
| HENRY | Er, right, the er . . . the village jumble sale. Should it be held on the 4th, or . . . |
| SUSAN | Yes! |
| HENRY | Oh. Right. 4th. Everyone agree? |
| SUSAN | Yes, they agree! |
| HENRY | Right. 4th. And should it be in the morning, or . . . |
| SUSAN | Yes! |
| HENRY | Oh. Right. Morning. Everyone . . . |

SUSAN         Yes, they agree!

HENRY         Right. 4th. In the morning. Right. That's er . . .

SUSAN         Is that it?

HENRY         Er . . . yes, that's it. Apart from any other business.

SUSAN         Anyone got any other business? No? Conclude the meeting, Henry.

HENRY         Er . . . meeting of the village-hall committee concluded.

SUSAN         Right. That's that, then. Sorry the food's not very inspiring this week. It's not been . . . you know . . .

LINDA         It's fine, honestly. Better than that Lisa would do. Lisa. (*She spits.*)

SUSAN         Yeah, Lisa. (*She spits. It accidentally goes into the quiche. The others all react.*) Oh my God, I'm so sorry. How embarrassing. I'll have that piece.

PETER         What do you mean that piece? It went all over.

LINDA         Oh, do be quiet. (*To* SUSAN.) So what are you going to do?

SUSAN         I don't know, stir it in a bit I suppose.

LINDA         I meant about Richard and the divorce.

SUSAN         Why should I give him a divorce? He hasn't made it easy for me, why should I make it easy for him? I've spent my whole life being helpful and supportive and considerate, and where has it got me?

HENRY         No, don't say that. I think you're a wonderful person.

| | |
|---|---|
| SUSAN | I've supported his career, I've raised his family, I've... I've... |
| LINDA | Had home-made bread on the table every other day. |
| SUSAN | Home-made bread on the table every other day. And you know what he used to say? "It's so homely. I love it." Well I'm sick of it. Homely. I'm stuck here being homely while he's off having Humpty Dumpty with some glamorous little trollop half my age. It's not homely he wants from her is it? I'll give him homely. I can be glamorous too, you know. Take off two or three pounds. |
| PETER | How many? |
| LINDA | (*whacking him*) She's got a lovely figure. Just needs a bit of toning here and there. (*To* SUSAN.) You come to my Stretch and Flow class, I'll get you sorted. |
| PETER | (*to* HENRY) Stretch and Flow she calls it. A more appropriate term would be Crunch and Groan. |
| LINDA | You'll be groaning in a minute. (*To* SUSAN.) Yes, you come to my class and get toned-up. |
| SUSAN | At the Stretch and Flow, with all the other pensioners. |
| LINDA | (*rising and moving to her*) No, no, I didn't mean that. You can come to my general keep-fit class, or my aerobics class if you'd prefer. I just thought... |
| SUSAN | You just thought I'd fit in better with the golden oldies. |
| LINDA | Tell you what, let's do one-to-one. Like a personal trainer. Yes, that's a much better idea. |

| | |
|---|---|
| | I'll soon get you toned-up. Yes, get yourself toned-up and get yourself a toy boy. |
| SUSAN | A toy boy? |
| LINDA | That'll show Richard. Show him he's not the only one that can get a bit of youthful action. Oh yes, I quite like this toy boy idea. Everybody's doing it these days you know. |
| PETER | Everybody? |
| LINDA | Well . . . so I've heard. I wouldn't know personally, of course. But I do think this could be the answer, Susan. If Richard's feeding his ego with that . . . that . . . Lisa . . . (*She spits.*) . . . then why shouldn't you get your ego fed? |
| HENRY | No, no, I hardly think that's the right course of action. |
| LINDA | It's perfect, Henry. Do her the world of good. Get her ego fed and her juices flowing. |
| HENRY | No, I'm sorry, but I really don't think . . . |
| SUSAN | (*crossing up to* HENRY) What, you don't think I could? |
| HENRY | No, it's not that . . . |
| SUSAN | You don't think I'm good enough for a toy boy? |
| HENRY | That's not what I'm saying. |
| SUSAN | If everyone else is doing it, why not me? Why shouldn't I get my juices fed? |
| LINDA | Flowing. |
| SUSAN | Flowing. Why couldn't I have a toy boy if I wanted one? I'm not saying I do want one, but if I did . . . |

| | |
|---|---|
| PETER | Just a minute, just a minute, let's not get ridiculous here. If you want my advice, forget the toy boy and just get yourself a dog. |
| SUSAN | Oh, thank you very much. |
| LINDA | Don't be so patronising. |
| PETER | Or a computer. Get on that net. (*To* HENRY.) That'll sort her juices out. |
| LINDA | (*looks at him*) How do you know about juicy nets? |
| PETER | It's just what I've heard. I wouldn't know personally, of course. |
| LINDA | Yes. Anyway, she's not interested in your advice. |
| SUSAN | I'm not interested in your advice. And why shouldn't I have a toy boy? I'm the right age for one. Fifty-six. |
| PETER | Fifty-eight. |
| SUSAN | Fifty-seven! |
| LINDA | So how old is this . . . Lisa? (*She spits.*) |
| SUSAN | Lisa. (*She spits.*) Thirty-six. |
| LINDA | Well just make sure your toy boy's younger than that. |
| SUSAN | Thirty-six. She's younger than our Jackie. (*She crosses and sits in the armchair.*) I've got a daughter who's coming up to forty. |
| LINDA | Now, now, no despair. Stay with the anger. |
| SUSAN | And she's proud to be forty. Keeps telling everyone. Why can't she be like any normal female and keep quiet about it? |

| | |
|---|---|
| LINDA | No despair, I said. |
| SUSAN | Oh this is all so stupid. Who am I kidding? |
| HENRY | (*he rises, crosses and sits on the sofa*) Susan. Forget about toy boys, forget about dogs and computers and forty-year-old daughters, just be happy with who you are. None of this is your fault. |
| SUSAN | Of course it's my fault. I'm obviously too frumpy and dumpy and homely. |
| THOMAS | Excuse me . . . could I say something, please? |
| SUSAN | Why not? Everyone else is having their say. |
| THOMAS | I think we're all going round in circles here. This situation needs some clarification, systematic analysis, and some resolving conclusions. |
| LINDA | We're talking about the break-up of a marriage here, not one of your mathematical broadsheets. |
| THOMAS | (*he rises and crosses to upstage centre*) But certain principles remain the same in any set of circumstances. There must be reason, logic, and progression, otherwise chaos reigns. Susan, forget everybody's advice, the most important part of this equation is you. Only you know how to solve this problem, no one else. |
| SUSAN | But I don't know how to solve this problem. |
| THOMAS | You solve this problem by being totally selfish and single-minded. Not an easy thing for you to do I know, you're probably the most unselfish person I've ever met . . . but drastic circumstances require drastic measures. And there's nothing wrong in being selfish now and again. |

LINDA: That's right. (*To* PETER.) Ask him.

PETER: What have I done now?

THOMAS: At this point, whatever you want to do you should do, and whatever you want to have you should have. Stop thinking about other people. Stop doing things for other people. Only do it if you want to do it. (*He moves down and sits on the sofa next to* HENRY.) Let me ask you something. At this moment in your life, given your current circumstances, what is it that you really want?

SUSAN: Another drink.

THOMAS: No, no, be serious.

SUSAN: I am being serious. And I'd like Sean Connery to serve it please.

PETER: I'll get it.

LINDA: God, what a letdown. Sean Connery to Boris Karloff in one fell swoop.

THOMAS: No, come on, it's systematic clarification we're looking for here. What do you want from your life at the moment? And think selfishly.

SUSAN: I don't know what I want.

THOMAS: Okay, let's find out then. Do you want your husband back?

SUSAN / HENRY: Look, I really don't think . . . / Now, now, look here . . .

THOMAS: No, no, let's see it through. Do you want him back or not?

SUSAN: No. Yes. No! I don't know.

HENRY: Can we stop this now, please?

THOMAS  I'm just trying to find out what she wants.

SUSAN  But I don't know what I want!

HENRY  She doesn't know what she wants.

THOMAS  Well keep asking the question. And until you do know what it is you want, every response should be a selfish one. (*He rises and heads to his place at the table.*) I think this should be put to the committee. The committee will help you. I put forward the motion that in her current situation, Susan should be totally selfish. All those in favour say aye. (*He raises his hand.*) Henry?

HENRY  Er...

THOMAS  That's near enough. Linda?

LINDA  Sorry, but I think revenge is the answer. All those in favour of revenge say "aye." (*She raises her hand.*)

HENRY  Revenge is not the answer to anything.

LINDA  Oh yes it is. And it fits perfectly with Thomas' theory. Revenge makes you feel better, and anything you do to make yourself feel better can most certainly be classed as a selfish act. (*To* SUSAN.) First, you get a toy boy to make Richard jealous, and then... I will be the instrument of a second bit of revenge for you.

SUSAN  A second bit of revenge?

LINDA  Yes. I will contrive to bump into Richard and... Lisa... (*She spits.*)... in the street, and I will pretend to be Richard's mistress.

PETER  Mistress?

| | |
|---|---|
| LINDA | Yes, mistress. You know what a mistress is. Something between a mister and a mattress. I will create a scene, and accuse him of not seeing me enough. He will protest his innocence . . . "but she's not a mistress, she's just a friend" . . . but the doubts will creep in. Dear little Lisa . . . (*She spits.*) . . . will start to get very worried. Good plan, don't you think? All those in favour? |
| HENRY | (*he rises and moves upstage centre*) No, I'm sorry, but I don't agree with that at all. If we're going to vote on anything, then let's vote that this wonderful person here stays as she is. I don't think she should change. All those in favour of her not changing? (*He raises his hand.*) |
| | (*They are now all around the table area facing away from* SUSAN.) |
| PETER | Hold on, hold on, this is getting us nowhere. Life is life, things happen, and sometimes there's nothing we can do about it. We just have to accept, and move on. And that's what I go for, acceptance and moving on. All those in favour? (*He raises his hand.*) |
| SUSAN | (*rising*) Excuse me. What is this, marriage guidance by committee? |
| PETER | (*crossing to her*) Acceptance Susan, that's the answer. Let's be honest . . . there is only one immutable truth in life, and that is . . . that some days you're the pigeon, and some days you're the statue. That's life. And it's no use fighting against it. At the moment you are a statue that is well and truly covered, but tomorrow . . . who knows? |
| LINDA | So that's your philosophy on life is it? |
| PETER | I learned that from Jung. |

| | |
|---|---|
| LINDA | Jung? Oh yes, I can just imagine Jung talking about pigeons and statues. |
| PETER | All I will say Susan, to finish this, is that we're your friends, and whatever you decide, we'll support you . . . and if you ever need anything from any of us . . . you only have to ask. |
| THOMAS | Hear, hear. |
| HENRY | Hear, hear. |
| LINDA | Hear, hear, too. |
| SUSAN | Thank you. Thank you very much, all of you. |
| PETER | And on that note, I suppose we ought to get going. Fancy a pint on the way Henry? |
| HENRY | Er . . . yes, that would be nice. |
| PETER | Thomas? |
| THOMAS | Just a quick one. |

(*The men collect their papers and folders.*)

| | |
|---|---|
| LINDA | (*to* PETER) I'll see you at home. I'm going to stay with Susan for a bit. |
| SUSAN | You don't have to stay . . . you go to the pub with them. I'll be all right. |
| LINDA | No, I'm fed up with pubs. All they ever talk about is football, cars, and politics. And every one of them knows how the country should be run . . . makes me die. Pubs are where you realise that men are like lava lamps. Fun to look at, but not very bright. (*To* PETER.) I'll give it a miss this time, and I'll see you at home later. |

(PETER, HENRY, *and* THOMAS *head for the front door.* SUSAN *opens the door for them.*)

| | |
|---|---|
| THOMAS | See you, Susan. And don't forget, stay selfish. |
| SUSAN | I'll try Thomas, I'll try. (THOMAS *leaves*.) |
| HENRY | Bye, Susan. Please don't change. I love you just the way you are. |
| PETER | You're starting to sound like Billy Joel, Henry. Come on, let's go. |
| SUSAN | Bye, Henry. (HENRY *leaves*.) |
| PETER | (*to* SUSAN) See you soon. And just remember what Jung said. |
| SUSAN | Pigeons and statues . . . how could I forget? Bye. (PETER *leaves*.) |
| | (SUSAN *closes the door behind them and heads back into the room.*) |
| | Linda, are you sure? I feel guilty keeping you here. |
| LINDA | Don't be so daft. I'd much rather have a drink here with you. If you don't mind, that is? |
| SUSAN | Of course I don't mind. |
| LINDA | Good. That's settled then. Give me your glass. |
| | (LINDA *takes* SUSAN's *glass and tops it up.*) |
| | Well, what an evening. What a phone call. I have to admit, I did love the bit about sticking his head in a winepress. And where the hell did winepress come from anyway? |
| SUSAN | God knows. All I could think of at the time. |
| LINDA | (*handing* SUSAN *her drink*) The dog mess was good too. |

SUSAN      Well that's how I feel. God, I'm so angry with him. How can he be so stupid? Oh, I'm sorry, I don't mean to go on.

LINDA      Don't be sorry. As I said, this is progress. This is the next stage.

(SUSAN *stops and looks at* LINDA.)

SUSAN      Oh, Linda . . . what am I going to do?

LINDA      I don't know. But it'll be all right, you'll see.

SUSAN      I don't want to be on my own. It frightens me, Linda.

LINDA      But you're not on your own. You've got Jackie, you've got your friends . . .

SUSAN      You know what I mean. (*She sits at the table.*)

LINDA      Well, maybe all is not lost. Maybe he'll change his mind . . . come to his senses. (*She sits at the table.*) Maybe it's not over yet.

SUSAN      It's over. The last vestige of hope I had was dashed with that phone call. He wants a divorce. Can't be more over than that. Oh, I'm sorry to be so negative, it's just that . . . it's just that I've never been on my own, and the thought of it terrifies me. I'm fifty-seven. What the hell am I going to do?

LINDA      Fifty-seven's not old. There's all sorts of things you can do. And I'm going to help you do them.

SUSAN      That's what makes me so angry. I get to this point, and I just feel I've wasted my life.

LINDA      Of course it's not been wasted.

SUSAN      You know how I feel? I feel my life stopped at eighteen. That's when I stopped living for me. I

|       | met Richard and we got engaged when I was seventeen. . . got pregnant, got married, and had Jackie when I was eighteen. From that point on my life was all about them. I just looked after them. I've never even had a proper job. Oh yes, I've been busy . . . committees, charities, racing round here and there . . . don't know where the time has gone . . . but it's all been about other people. It's not been about me. |
|-------|---|
| LINDA | It has been about you. And you've done wonderful things. Helped so many people. |
| SUSAN | Got taken advantage of you mean. |
| LINDA | And please don't say it's been a waste, because it hasn't. Look at that wonderful daughter of yours. That's an incredible achievement in itself. |
| SUSAN | Of course I don't regret having Jackie, she's the joy of my life . . . but I was eighteen. Sowed one wild oat and that was it. What the hell do I know about anything? The supposed Swinging Sixties that was. Swinging, huh? Swinging Jackie on my hip and swinging her in the playground, that's what it meant to me. One wild oat. Pathetic, eh? I've been faithful for thirty-nine years, and look where it's got me. (*She sits on the sofa.*) |
| LINDA | It's never too late to sow wild oats, you know. |
| SUSAN | I wouldn't know where to start . . . or how. Fifty-seven and no experience. Some admission that is. |
| LINDA | So was Richard the only . . . you know . . . |
| SUSAN | No, no, he was the first meaningful one. The first time was with a spotty boy called Steven Wilkins. Just a bit of a fumble really. We did it, but I don't think he got it right. |

| | |
|---|---|
| LINDA | Yeah well, that's life. Most men never do get it right. Even when you tell them. (*She looks at* SUSAN.) Faithful for thirty-nine years. Some going, that is. That's almost noble. |
| SUSAN | Noble? Downright bloody stupid, you mean. I wish now I'd taken some of those opportunities that came my way. |
| LINDA | You had opportunities? |
| SUSAN | Don't look so surprised. I've had opportunities. Opportunities and propositions. Oh yes. (*She stops.*) Mostly from blokes I didn't fancy, of course. Why does that always happen? Why does it have to be this one, why can't it be that gorgeous one over there? Life, I suppose. I did have a couple of really close ones though. |
| LINDA | Did you? |
| SUSAN | Long time ago. |
| LINDA | Well? Come on, then. |
| SUSAN | No, no, it was all too long ago. |
| LINDA | Have another drink. (*She hurries across, takes* SUSAN's *glass and tops it up.*) So, come on, who were they? Come on. |
| | (SUSAN *looks at her and makes the decision to tell her.*) |
| SUSAN | You'll die when you hear about the first one. |
| LINDA | Let me die, let me die. |
| SUSAN | (*she rises, crosses and collects her glass*) We were on holiday in Greece. Jackie was ten, and she and Richard decided to go on this two-day island-hopping excursion, which I didn't fancy. They were happy to go without me, and as |

| | |
|---|---|
| | soon as they'd left, I signed up for a scuba diving lesson. |
| LINDA | I thought you hated swimming? |
| SUSAN | I do. But the instructor was the most beautiful man I had ever seen. He really stirred things up in me . . . you know that feeling? |
| LINDA | Yes dear, I know that feeling very well. |
| SUSAN | I just thought . . . I don't care if I drown. I told him I wasn't too confident in the water, so he told me to stay close to him. When we were under, I kept panicking and grabbing him . . . which was a bit disconcerting for him, obviously . . . with all those pipes and tubes sticking out everywhere . . . it was awful . . . and with these huge tight goggles almost sucking my eyes out. But I didn't care. Anyway, somehow I survived, and afterwards we ended up having a drink together . . . we were laughing a lot, I remember . . . God he was beautiful . . . and I was like a schoolgirl, giggling, crossing my legs, panting, laughing at all of his jokes . . . it was wonderful. He then invited me for a drink in his room. I said I'd just nip back and sort myself out, and that I'd meet him in his room shortly. I got back to my room, nervous, excited . . . couldn't believe what I was doing, I'd never lusted like that before . . . and then . . . then . . . I caught sight of myself in the mirror. I had these huge black marks round my eyes where the goggles had been. Huge. I looked like the Panda from Hell. He'd obviously been too polite to say anything. Well . . . first it was a shock, then it made me laugh, then it embarrassed me, then it upset me, then it made me cry, and then . . . it brought me back to earth. |
| LINDA | Oh, no. |
| SUSAN | I just phoned his room . . . and bottled out. |

LINDA: Oh, no. I can't bear it!

SUSAN: Like a stupid schoolgirl.

LINDA: Didn't you try again? You had two days.

SUSAN: The moment had passed. Of course the way I feel now, I wish I had gone through with it.

LINDA: So do I. God . . . lost opportunities. So who was the second one? You said there were a couple.

SUSAN: No one knows about that one.

LINDA: It's all right, your secret's safe with me. (SUSAN *just looks at her.*) All right, I'll do my best, okay?

SUSAN: No, no . . . I'm not sure that I should.

LINDA: Come on, you can't stop now.

(*She looks at* LINDA.)

SUSAN: It was Henry.

LINDA: Henry? (SUSAN *nods.*) What, our Henry?

SUSAN: He's always had a thing about me. And there was an occasion . . . we had a chance . . . we'd always fought against it . . . but there was this time . . . it was so lovely . . . we kissed . . . and then . . .

LINDA: What, what?

SUSAN: I started crying.

LINDA: Oh, no, not crying again, please don't tell me that.

SUSAN: And we stopped. And we never got to that point again. He then married Elizabeth . . . and

| | |
|---|---|
| | we both tried to pretend it had never happened . . . but I knew he still . . . |
| LINDA | So you never . . . |
| SUSAN | No. It was one of those moments you know? My whole life could have changed. He was so dashing in those days . . . so handsome, so romantic, so caring . . . and he loved me so much. And I loved him. And I didn't take the moment. I was loyal. I was stupid. And now look what's happened. Bloody men. |
| LINDA | Yeah, bloody men. I'll drink to that. (*They raise their glasses.*) Bloody men! |
| SUSAN | Bloody men! |
| | (*They drink.*) |
| LINDA | Do you think we really need men? |
| SUSAN | I don't know, I've always had one. |
| LINDA | I suppose we do need them. They can be quite nice in certain circumstances. Maybe it's not men as such, maybe it's the system that's wrong. It's the person who invented marriage, he's the cause of all the problems. We need a different way. Like a rota system or something. Yes, that's it, a rota system. Get one that's good at DIY and heavy lifting, one to take you out wining and dining, one that's a good listener, one that likes children, and three or four that are wonderful lovers. Whatever your mood, whatever your need, you just phone up the appropriate one. Now why couldn't that work? |
| SUSAN | No reason at all. Sounds a wonderful idea. |
| LINDA | And also, if marriage is supposed to be a union, why can't it be run like a union? The right to strike, proper pay and working |

conditions, decent hours, redundancy pay . . . and if they decide to walk out on you, they should first set you up with a temp. Marriage just complicates everything. It was all very easy in the cavemen days. You just got bonked on the head, dragged by the hair, and got bonked again. All very straightforward, you knew where you stood.

SUSAN  Can you please not use that awful expression. I hate the word bonk.

LINDA  I've always thought it depends on who's doing it. If it was George Clooney, he could call it what he liked.

SUSAN  It's such an uninvolving word. Why can't we just make love?

LINDA  Because that's not always what we're doing.

SUSAN  Well I want another expression.

LINDA  There's already plenty of other expressions. Night-time tango.

SUSAN  Oh yes, that's quite nice. And during the day?

LINDA  During the day? Now there's a novelty. Er . . . daytime dalliance, early-morning uprising, lunchtime lunging, afternoon aerobics, broom-cupboard rumba, back-seat bossa-nova, kitchen-table can-can.

SUSAN  Kitchen-table? Oh God, my poor back. (*They laugh.*) Want another drink?

LINDA  No thanks. I'd better make a move.

SUSAN  (*stopping her*) Linda, Thank you so much. You've been such a help.

LINDA  Look, I know it's difficult, but maybe it's a good thing. A new start. It doesn't have to be

|  | negative. (*She rises and collects her papers from the table.*) People do all sorts of things at all sorts of ages. It's never too late to fall in love, it's never too late to write a book, sail round the world, start a career . . . get a toy boy . . . all sorts of things. And it's never too late to dream either. |
|---|---|
| SUSAN | It is for me. Last time I felt like that was eighteen. When I was eighteen, I had dreams in my heart and wings on my feet. I could have done anything. |
| LINDA | You still can. Those dreams haven't gone away, they just haven't happened yet, that's all. You just have to stop being afraid. |
| SUSAN | Easy to be fearless when you're young. |
| LINDA | Talk to me, let me help, and I promise we'll get through this. |
| SUSAN | Oh Linda, I don't want this. |
| LINDA | Of course you don't. You want something better. And I'm going to help you get it. Come here. (*They hug.*) I'll call you tomorrow. Okay? |
| SUSAN | Okay. |
| LINDA | (*heading for the door*) Bye. And remember, stay angry, and retain vengeful thoughts. And try to think of something slightly more accessible than an industrial winepress. Stay strong my Susan, you're heading for a better life. See you. |
|  | (LINDA *leaves.*) |
| SUSAN | Bye. (*She closes the door behind her, picks up her drink and heads for the sofa.*) Something better. Yes. That's what I want. Something better. (*She sits on the sofa.*) Here's to you Susan Shaw. And here's to a better life. |

*(She takes a drink and then, after a few moments, she starts to gently sob. The lights fade. End of Scene One.)*

### Scene Two

*It is a week later.* HENRY, PETER, LINDA, THOMAS *and* SUSAN *are seated round the table. Another meeting is in progress.* SUSAN *and* LINDA *are both wearing tracksuits.*

HENRY  And finally, just to inform you that we made a profit on the Bring and Buy sale. Thomas.

THOMAS  Yes. After all our expenses, we made the princely sum of £164.52p.

PETER  Doesn't sound very much.

THOMAS  But it is, considering this is pure profit made over a period of three hours. This surpassed my projected forecast, and statistically speaking, compared to previous events of this nature, bringing into account percentage probabilities of numbers attending and average spending capacity, the ratio of profit against time materialised very favourably, bearing in mind that certain factors involved in the equation can at times be unpredictable, and therefore not always subject to normal statistical analysis. Saying that, however, I am encouraged . . .

PETER  *(jumping in)* So am I, Thomas, so am I. You win. I agree. It is indeed a princely sum.

THOMAS  Oh good, I'm glad you think so. And because of the success of this event, the suggestion is that we hold another in three months' time.

HENRY  That's right. And thank you, Thomas, for your clarity in this matter. We'll confirm dates at the

|  |  |
|---|---|
|  | next meeting. Right. Well, that's the last item on the agenda . . . er . . . any other business? |
| SUSAN | (*raising her hand*) Yes! I have some any other business. |
| HENRY | Oh, right. |
| SUSAN | I would just like to inform the committee that we won't be using my house for meetings any more. |
| HENRY | Oh. |
| SUSAN | Someone else can have the hassle. |
| HENRY | Oh. |
| SUSAN | Someone else can provide the food and drink. |
| HENRY | Oh. Well, this is er . . . this is a bit of a surprise, Susan. Is everything all right? |
| SUSAN | Everything's fine, thank you, Henry. |
| HENRY | Yes . . . well we have been using your house a lot . . . |
| SUSAN | That's right, you have. |
| HENRY | . . . and we do realise it is extra work for you . . . |
| SUSAN | That's right, it is. |
| HENRY | . . . and we're aware there must be a modicum of inconvenience . . . |
| SUSAN | That's right, there is. |
| HENRY | . . . and I hope you don't feel we've taken advantage, it's just that . . . well, you did offer. |
| SUSAN | That's right, I did. And now I'm retracting the offer. |

| | |
|---|---|
| HENRY | I see. Right. Well, we er . . . we need to decide where the next meeting's going to be held. |
| LINDA | (*to* PETER) We could use our place. |
| PETER | Yeah. Yeah, that'd be okay. I could do the food if you like. |
| LINDA | Oh, no you won't. He learned to cook from his mother. She's the sort that uses the smoke detector as a meal timer. |
| SUSAN | I'm sorry if my announcement has thrown you all . . . but I've decided to follow your advice Thomas. From now on I'm going to be totally selfish. |
| THOMAS | Oh, that's great. |
| SUSAN | (*rises and moves round behind them*) Yes. I am going to learn the spelling and the meaning of the word "no." I'm not going to do anything I don't want to do, I'm just going to think about me. |
| THOMAS | Good for you. |
| HENRY | Er, Susan . . . I don't think . . . |
| SUSAN | I'm also going to follow your advice, Henry. |
| HENRY | Oh. |
| SUSAN | You don't want me to change, well I'm not going to change, exactly. I'm going to be me, but I'm going to be a different me. I'm going to be more like the me I was at eighteen. Is that okay for you? |
| HENRY | Er . . . I think so. |
| SUSAN | I'm also going to follow your advice, Linda. |
| LINDA | Oh, good. |

**SUSAN**   Revenge is now on the agenda. Can't see the harm in a few vengeful acts . . . make me feel better. Selfish I know . . . but that's the point of the exercise. Peter.

**PETER**   Yes!

**SUSAN**   I agree with you that I should accept the unpredictability of life, but what I will not accept is this statue business. From now on I intend to be the pigeon.

**PETER**   Attagirl!

**SUSAN**   So thank you dear friends for all your valued advice, I shall follow it gladly. And I'm sorry again about not using my house for meetings, but I'm going to be rather busy doing things for me. And as you can probably gather from my attire . . . the first thing I'm going to be busy with . . . is my very own personal trainer.

**LINDA**   (*putting her hand up*) That's me! As you can probably gather from my attire, too.

**SUSAN**   As soon as the meeting's over, we're going to make a start. I've decided I'd like to get toned-up.

**LINDA**   Yes. We're going to get her toned-up, and then we're going to get her a toy boy.

**SUSAN**   I've not decided about the toy boy yet. In fact, I've not decided about men at all. As far as I can see they're more trouble than they're worth.

**PETER**   Oh, thanks very much.

**SUSAN**   Present company included of course.

**PETER**   Don't you mean excluded?

**LINDA**   She knows what she means.

SUSAN        Things are going to be very different from now on. If I don't want to make damson jam for the WI, then I won't. If I don't want to work once or twice a week in the Help The Aged, then I won't. No more of this, "oh, just ask Susan, she'll do it. She'll do anything for anyone. She'll do the food, she'll do the coffee mornings, she'll do the organising, she'll do the running round." Well, no more. No more Mrs Nice Girl! The new me has arisen from the shackles of charities and committees. So take care people, the pigeon is loose! (*She moves round to confront them.*) And the pigeon has potential, the pigeon has dreams . . . and the pigeon is not stupid. (*She looks at them.*) Is she?

(*The others jump up and quickly say "no."*)

Right. That's that settled, then. (*She sits back in her place.*)

HENRY        Yes. Well . . . er . . . moving on. Any more any other business?

SUSAN        (*raising her hand*) Yes! I have some more any other business.

HENRY        Oh, right.

SUSAN        (*rises and gets invites from the sideboard drawer*) It will shortly be my fifty-eighth birthday, and you are all cordially invited to the party I'll be holding. Here are your invites. (*She hands out the invites to them and sits back in her place.*)

HENRY        Thank you, Susan. Right, well er . . . any more any other business?

SUSAN        (*raising her hand*) Yes! I have one more item of any other business. (*She rises and moves across centre.*) This refers back to the subject

|  |  |
|--|--|
| | of revenge. Can anybody tell me . . . does voodoo work on objects? |
| HENRY | Sorry? |
| SUSAN | I mean, I know you can stick pins in people, but I don't actually want to hurt the person or persons involved . . . although I do consider I would have every right to do so . . . and I was just wondering . . (*She moves round to confront them again.*) . . . if you stuck a pin in the tyre of a model car, for example . . . (*She looks at them.*) . . . what do you think?<br><br>(*They are just staring at her.*)<br><br>Anyone here versed in voodoo?<br><br>(*They continue to stare.*)<br><br>No? Just a thought. Right. (*She sits back in her place.*) Anyone else have any other business?<br><br>(*They all shake their heads.*)<br><br>Conclude the meeting, Henry. |
| HENRY | Er . . . Village Hall Committee meeting concluded. |
| SUSAN | Right. Sorry there's no food and drink this evening, you'll just have to make do with the pub. I've got toning-up to do.<br><br>(*They continue to stare.*)<br><br>Off you go, then.<br><br>(*They start to get up, not quite sure. She bangs on the table and heads for the door.*)<br><br>Come on, come on! Haven't got all night! |

(THOMAS, PETER and HENRY *quickly get themselves together.*)

If I don't see you before, I'll see you at my party.

THOMAS  Susan, I think you're very . . .

SUSAN  That's very sweet of you, Thomas. Bye now. (*She gently pushes him out.*)

HENRY  Susan . . .

SUSAN  See you soon, Henry. (*She gently pushes him out.*)

PETER  Susan . . .

SUSAN  Bye, Peter. (*She gently pushes him out. She closes the door behind them and moves back into the room.*)

Oh God, was that terrible of me?

LINDA  Now, now, don't start the guilt. This is the new selfish you, remember?

SUSAN  Yes, yes you're right. The new selfish me. Want a drink?

LINDA  No, let's get started. We'll have a drink later. Come on, help me with this. (*They move the table upstage.*) Right, tracksuits off.

(*They take off their tracksuits.* LINDA *is in stylish leotard and tights,* SUSAN *is in leggings, slightly too short, and a baggy sweat shirt.*)

SUSAN  Oh, God, look at me. I've put on so much weight.

LINDA  Now, now, now, I don't want language like that. Remember, a woman does not put on

|  |  |
|---|---|
|  | weight, she is merely a metabolic underachiever. |
| SUSAN | It's all a load of metabolics these days. |
|  | (LINDA *takes a CD from her exercise bag that is set next to the sideboard and goes to the CD player.*) |
| LINDA | We'll start gently, okay? Don't want to go too mad first time out. Okay, shall we have a go? |
| SUSAN | Ready when you are. |
|  | (LINDA *starts the music.*) |
| LINDA | Just follow me. |
|  | (*They go into a warm-up routine – shoulder rolls, arm circles, thigh bends and twisting from the waist.* SUSAN *is always slightly behind. At the end of this short routine,* LINDA *stops.*) |
| LINDA | Well done, that was good. |
| SUSAN | That was good. Want a drink now? |
| LINDA | A drink? No, that was just the warm-up. |
| SUSAN | The warm-up?. |
|  | (LINDA *turns the music off.*) |
| LINDA | Right, let's get the steps. (*She gets the two steps that are set beside her exercise bag and they place them in position for the class.*) Different music this time. (*She turns the music on. It is an 'insistent' exercise beat.*) Here we go. Follow me . . . to the right . . . and . . . |
|  | (*This first exercise is stepping to the right and left.*) |

|         | Oh yes, we'll get that body toned-up, don't you worry. You'll be fighting them off soon. |
|---------|---|
| SUSAN   | This isn't just about men, you know. |
| LINDA   | It's always about men. |
| SUSAN   | This is to make me feel better about myself. |
| LINDA   | And it will make you feel better. Get all those juices flowing again. It'll revitalise your sex life, too. |
| SUSAN   | I don't have a sex life. I have hot-water bottles. |
| LINDA   | Oh we'll soon change that. Right, here we go . . . and . . . back . . . |

(*They start moving backwards and forwards.*)

| SUSAN | Oh God, where are we going now? |
|---|---|
| LINDA | Watch my arm movements. That's it, that's it. |
| SUSAN | And anyway, sex isn't the be-all and end-all of everything. |
| LINDA | Don't kid yourself. Sex is like air. It's not important until you're not getting any. I'll also introduce you to a friend of mine from work. You'll like him, he's absolutely disgraceful. |
| SUSAN | I'm not interested in your leftovers, thank you very much. |
| LINDA | You'll be interested in this one all right. Every time you tell him not to do something, he does it. So delicious. Right, here we go . . . to the sides . . . and . . . |

(*They start stepping right and left again, this time with different arm movements.*)

| | |
|---|---|
| LINDA | Then we'll get the hair seen to. Start using make-up. |
| SUSAN | I don't like make-up. And what's wrong with my hair? |
| LINDA | Nothing. We just have to maximise the potential, that's all. Remember, you're a woman. You must use all weapons available. You're the brighter sex, you're tough, and you have the control. |
| SUSAN | I don't feel in control. |
| LINDA | We women always have control. Listen, when a man goes out on a date he wonders if he's going to get lucky. The woman already knows. That's control. Right, here we go . . . step-ups . . . and . . . |

(*They start doing step-ups onto the steps.*)

| | |
|---|---|
| SUSAN | This is doing me good, isn't it? |
| LINDA | Of course. |
| SUSAN | Just checking. So you think we're the brighter sex do you? |
| LINDA | Of course we are. I mean, you know what they say. Diamonds are a girl's best friend, dogs are a man's best friend. You tell me who's the brighter sex. And tough. You've got to be tough. |
| SUSAN | Yeah, got to be tough. |
| LINDA | No more being taken advantage of. No more fear. Get tough. |
| SUSAN | Yeah, get tough. |
| LINDA | Like my grandmother. Now there was tough woman. Do you know she buried three |

husbands. And two of them were just having a nap. Here we go . . . to the back . . . and . . .

(*They start moving backwards and forwards again.*)

Oh yes, it's great to be a woman. You're not expected to know how cars work, you don't have to understand the offside rule, you look better naked than men, you don't need an excuse to be in a bad mood, and you don't have to constantly adjust your genitals. It's just great!

(*The doorbell rings.*)

SUSAN  Is that the doorbell? I thought I heard the doorbell.

(*She moves up and turns the music off.*)

LINDA  And we were doing so well.

SUSAN  (*heading for the door*) I'm sure I heard it.

(*Her movements are slightly stiff, she looks exhausted and her hair is rather dishevelled as she opens the door.*)

Thomas.

(THOMAS *steps in.*)

THOMAS  I wonder if I could have a quick word.

SUSAN  Well . . . er, we're in the middle of a class.

THOMAS  I realise that, and I'm sorry, but . . .

SUSAN  Is something wrong, Thomas? What's happened?

THOMAS  No, no, nothing's wrong. And I promise I won't keep you long.

| | |
|---|---|
| SUSAN | Can't it wait? |
| THOMAS | I do need to say something to you . . . and I do need to say it now. It is rather important. |
| SUSAN | I see. Well . . . you'd better come in then. |
| | (THOMAS *moves into the room and* SUSAN *closes the door.*) |
| THOMAS | Sorry, Linda . . . about the interruption. |
| LINDA | That's okay. |
| SUSAN | Sit down, Thomas. |
| | (*The three of them sit down.* THOMAS *sits in the armchair*, SUSAN *and* LINDA *on the sofa.*) |
| SUSAN | Now, what could possibly be this urgent? |
| THOMAS | (*looking at* LINDA) Er . . . well . . . I think it needs to be private. |
| SUSAN | That's all right, we won't tell anyone. |
| THOMAS | No, no, it's just . . . (*He looks at* LINDA.) . . . I need to say it . . . (*He looks at* SUSAN.) . . . you know . . . to you. |
| SUSAN | Oh. Oh, I see. |
| LINDA | Oh. Oh, I see. Right, well I'll go and . . . do something. (*She heads into the kitchen.*) Excuse me. |
| THOMAS | Sorry. It's just that if I don't say it now I might never say it. Might lose my nerve. |
| SUSAN | So, what is it, Thomas? |
| THOMAS | Well . . . (*He rises, crosses and checks that* LINDA *has gone.*) . . . I've collated all the data |

|         |                                                                                                                                                                                                                   |
| ------- | ----------------------------------------------------------------------------------------------------------------------------------------------------------------------------------------------------------------- |
|         | in my mind, weighed up the probabilities and the possibilities, evaluated the percentages of a possible positive outcome, and feel that my proposition is on firm enough ground to make a calculated progression. |
| SUSAN   | I see. And in English?                                                                                                                                                                                            |
| THOMAS  | I've weighed up the pros and cons. So I'd like to say that er . . . er . . .                                                                                                                                      |
| SUSAN   | Yes?                                                                                                                                                                                                              |
| THOMAS  | Er . . . that er . . . that er . . .                                                                                                                                                                              |
| SUSAN   | Yes?                                                                                                                                                                                                              |
| THOMAS  | . . . that er . . . should you be giving the matter serious consideration, I would like to nominate myself for the possible forthcoming position of toy boy.                                                      |
| SUSAN   | Sorry?                                                                                                                                                                                                            |
| THOMAS  | I'm willing, I'm able, I'm healthy, and I'm available. I've always been very taken by the charms, the experience, and the understanding of some older women . . . and I certainly do find you very attractive . . . |
|         | (SUSAN *looks at herself.*)                                                                                                                                                                                       |
| SUSAN   | Really?                                                                                                                                                                                                           |
| THOMAS  | . . . so if you were going to pursue that course of action, then I'd like to be put on your list of contenders.                                                                                                   |
| SUSAN   | I see.                                                                                                                                                                                                            |
| THOMAS  | And I'd also like to say that I will respect your decision, whatever that may be, and even if the answer is in the negative, I want to assure you                                                                 |

                    that it will in no way affect our friendship. (*He sits on the sofa beside her.*)

SUSAN               Right. Well, Thomas, I think what you've just said was meant to be flattering . . . and I thank you for that . . . but the first thing to say in matters like these, is that your romantic proposition shouldn't really have the feel of a job application. Matters of the romantic are a little more delicate and sensitive than that.

THOMAS              I see. Was that a yes or a no?

SUSAN               We're not there yet, Thomas. Men and women are very different. They require different approaches. Impressing a woman romantically can be a very complicated process. It requires a certain . . .

THOMAS              So how do you impress a woman?

SUSAN               How do you impress a woman? Well . . . well it's not always easy. She needs . . . er . . . well . . . you er, you compliment her, cuddle her, kiss her, caress her, love her, tease her, comfort her, protect her, hug her, hold her, spend money on her, wine and dine her, listen to her, care for her, stand by her, support her, and be prepared to go to the ends of the earth for her. That's how you impress a woman.

THOMAS              I see. And how do you impress a man?

SUSAN               That's easy. Turn up naked with beer. There are differences, Thomas.

THOMAS              Yes . . . yes, this is all very interesting. I'll try and be more impressive.

SUSAN               Don't try to do anything Thomas. I thank you for your kind offer, I am very flattered, and should I be thinking along those lines, then I will certainly give it due consideration.

| | |
|---|---|
| THOMAS | Right. Was that a yes or a no? |
| SUSAN | We're still not there yet, Thomas, but let's just say that the probability of me taking a toy boy at all, percentage wise, is at present highly unlikely. |
| THOMAS | Right. |
| SUSAN | And now I really should get on with my class. |
| THOMAS | Yes, of course. |

(*They get up and head for the door.*)

Oh, I've just remembered. I can do this.

(*He does something physically odd – double-jointed thumb maybe, or wiggling his ears.*)

| | |
|---|---|
| SUSAN | Thank you, Thomas, but I have to tell you, in the greater scheme of romantic matters, that is not altogether too impressive. |
| THOMAS | Right. Right, bye then. |
| SUSAN | Bye. (*She closes the door.*) Linda! |

(LINDA *enters from the kitchen.*)

| | |
|---|---|
| LINDA | What was all that about? |
| SUSAN | Oh, nothing serious. Shall we get on? |
| LINDA | Oh no you don't. Come on, it's me you're talking to. |
| SUSAN | I really don't think I ought to discuss it. It's a personal matter. |
| LINDA | Personal matters are the only things to discuss. |
| SUSAN | I'm not going into detail, suffice to say that I've just had a rather extraordinary offer. |

| | |
|---|---|
| LINDA | An offer? What sort of offer? |
| SUSAN | Just an offer. |
| LINDA | You mean . . . a personal offer? |
| SUSAN | Yes. |
| LINDA | From Thomas? |
| SUSAN | Yes. |
| LINDA | From Thomas. (*She looks at* SUSAN.) You mean . . . a toy boy-type offer? |
| SUSAN | Can we just get on please? |
| LINDA | Well I never. Thomas the toy boy. So what are you going to do? |
| SUSAN | Start the class. |

(*She turns the music on and returns to her position in front of her step.*)

| | |
|---|---|
| LINDA | To the right . . . and . . . (*They start stepping right and left again.*) Not really archetypical toy boy material though, is he? |
| SUSAN | I didn't mention toy boy, you did. |
| LINDA | Shouldn't they be like Greek Gods? He's more like a Greek salad. |
| SUSAN | Don't be so mean, he's very nice. |
| LINDA | Yes, but you don't want nice in a toy boy. You want mean and moody and rippling six-packs. |
| SUSAN | Oh that's easy to find then. |
| LINDA | Tousled hair and tight bums. Oh, God. |
| SUSAN | Can we change the subject please? |

| | |
|---|---|
| LINDA | I think we'd better. All this talk of mean and moody firm young flesh is making me feel quite sideways. Here we go . . . step-ups . . . and . . . |

(*They start step-ups again.*)

| | |
|---|---|
| SUSAN | Oh, God. |
| LINDA | Come on, keep up. |
| SUSAN | Keep up? I'm lucky I'm standing up. |
| LINDA | Just can't get over Thomas. Never thought he had it in him. So what was his chat-up routine like? |
| SUSAN | Mathematically expansive and romantically inept. |
| LINDA | Eh? |
| SUSAN | Oh no, I didn't mean to say that, how horrible of me. He was very sweet. |
| LINDA | Best chat-up line I had was just last week. I was standing outside the chemist and this bloke said to me, "Do you believe in love at first sight, or shall I walk past again?" Not bad, eh? |

(*The doorbell rings.*)

| | |
|---|---|
| SUSAN | The doorbell? Oh thank God for that. |

(SUSAN *turns off the music and struggles to the door, looking even more exhausted and dishevelled.*)

| | |
|---|---|
| LINDA | If it's a young Greek God, let him in. |

(SUSAN *opens the door.*)

| | |
|---|---|
| SUSAN | Henry. |

| | |
|---|---|
| LINDA | Ah well, never mind. |

(HENRY *steps in.*)

| | |
|---|---|
| HENRY | Sorry, but I wonder if I could have a quick word? |
| SUSAN | Er . . . I'm in the middle of a class, Henry. |
| HENRY | Yes, I realise that . . . sorry . . . it's just . . . |
| SUSAN | Is everything all right? |
| HENRY | Yes, yes, everything's fine. And I promise I won't keep you too long. |
| SUSAN | It can't wait, obviously? |
| HENRY | Well . . . it is rather important. |
| SUSAN | You'd better come in, then. |

(HENRY *moves into the room and* SUSAN *closes the door.*)

| | |
|---|---|
| HENRY | Sorry to interrupt, Linda. |
| LINDA | No no, I'm enjoying the intrigue. |
| SUSAN | Sit down, Henry. |

(*The three of them sit down,* LINDA *getting there first.* HENRY *sits in the armchair.*)

| | |
|---|---|
| SUSAN | So Henry, what can I do for you? |
| HENRY | Well . . . it's er . . . rather private. |
| SUSAN | I thought it might be. |
| LINDA | I thought it might be, too. |
| HENRY | Yes. It's er . . . personal. |

SUSAN — I thought it might be.

LINDA — I thought it might be, too.

HENRY — Right.

SUSAN — Right.

LINDA — Right. Well I'll go and er . . . do something else. (*She heads off into the kitchen.*) Excuse me.

SUSAN — So Henry . . .

HENRY — (*he rises and moves behind the sofa to centre*) Well . . . I have something to say, and if I don't say it now . . . it's just that I'd like to say that er . . . er . . .

SUSAN — Yes?

HENRY — . . . that er . . . that er . . .

SUSAN — Yes?

HENRY — . . . well, all this talk of you changing, Susan, I don't want you to change. I mean, I don't think you should change.

SUSAN — I told you earlier Henry, I'm not changing, exactly, I'm just . . .

HENRY — But you are, and I don't think you should. You are a very special person, with wonderful qualities. No set of circumstances and no other person should make you feel you have to be any different than you are. You are far, far better than any of them, and they don't deserve you.

SUSAN — Henry . . .

HENRY — Well . . . he doesn't deserve you, that's what I really mean. There. I've said it.

| | |
|---|---|
| SUSAN | Look, this is very nice of you, Henry... |
| HENRY | I'm not trying to be nice, Susan. (*He moves round and sits on the sofa next to her.*) You know how I feel about you. At least, I hope you do. |
| SUSAN | Yes, Henry, I do. |
| HENRY | It's how I've always felt about you. I never stopped. I just want you to know that I love you just as you are, warts and all. |
| SUSAN | Warts? What warts? |
| HENRY | I could look after you Susan, I could care for you, support you... |
| SUSAN | Henry, you must stop saying these things. |
| HENRY | Please don't stop me. Every day I want to say these things to you. If you were mine... |
| SUSAN | But I can't be yours, Henry, you're a married man. |
| HENRY | Elizabeth and I have led such separate lives, you know we have. We should never have got married in the first place. (*He stops and looks at her.*) Susan, I know we missed our chance... and I've regretted it every day since... but it's not too late, Susan, it's never too late. |
| SUSAN | Oh, Henry... |
| HENRY | I just wanted you to know. I wanted you to be certain of me. |
| SUSAN | Henry... |
| HENRY | No, you don't have to say anything. I just knew if I didn't tell you how I felt... I'd have another huge regret to live with. Susan, I don't want you to change. You're beautiful. |

(SUSAN *looks at herself.*)

SUSAN: Really?

HENRY: Really. Right. I've said what I wanted to say, so I'd er . . . I'd better leave you to your lesson. (*They rise and head for the door.*) And perhaps after you've had a little time to think, maybe we could talk again.

SUSAN: Yes, yes of course.

HENRY: (*stopping at the door*) I love you, Susan. I've always loved you. And I wanted you to know that I wanted you to know that. Right. Well, er . . . bye.

SUSAN: Bye. (*He heads off.* SUSAN *closes the door. She moves into the room, stops, and looks at herself.*) I should look like this more often. Linda!

(LINDA *enters from the kitchen.*)

LINDA: Well?

SUSAN: Oh . . . nothing really. Shall we get on?

LINDA: Don't start that again.

SUSAN: No, no, this was . . . this was a bit more serious . . . I think.

LINDA: Come on, you can't leave me in the air like this.

SUSAN: I'm sorry, really . . . let's just get going. Please.

(*She turns the music on, and they resume the stepping right and left exercise.*)

LINDA: Obviously another offer then? (SUSAN *doesn't reply.*) Well, it's always very nice for a lady to get an offer. Two offers in the space of ten minutes, however, is bordering on the obscene. Especially to that person's best friend who hasn't had a decent offer in months. Not even an indecent offer. Can't make men out sometimes. Here am I, physically prepared to be nimble and naughty and there's not even a sniff, and there's you, physically knackered and totally disinterested and the offers come flooding in. So what's that mean, then?

SUSAN   It wasn't an offer as such . . . more a declaration.

LINDA   Right, here we go . . . step-ups . . . and . . .

(*They start doing step-ups.*)

SUSAN   Oh, God.

LINDA   Offers and declarations, eh? I think it's great. A new journey, a new adventure . . . who knows what might happen? A leap into the dark!

SUSAN   I think I'd prefer a leap into the bath.

LINDA   Right, now we're doing punches . . . (*She starts a boxing-type punching exercise.*) Here we go . . . punches . . . and . . .

SUSAN   Oh, my God, what's this? (*She starts punching.*)

LINDA   Don't worry, this is the last bit. Oh yes, you're going to have fun! Now come on. say after me, . . . "Sod 'em all, we're young enough, it's never too late, to strut our stuff!" Come on . . . "Sod 'em all . . ."

SUSAN   "Sod 'em all," . . .

LINDA   . . . "we're young enough," . . .

SUSAN   . . . "we're young enough," . . .

| | |
|---|---|
| LINDA | ... "it's never too late," ... |
| SUSAN | ... "it's never too late," ... |
| LINDA | ... "to strut our stuff." |
| SUSAN | ... "to strut our stuff." |
| LINDA | "Sod 'em all, we're young enough, it's never too late, to strut our stuff." Come on! |

(LINDA *encourages* SUSAN *to join in, and they end up doing it together.*)

| | |
|---|---|
| LINDA / SUSAN | (*together*) "Sod 'em all, we're young enough, it's never too late, to strut our stuff. Sod 'em all, we're young enough, it's never too late, to strut our stuff." |
| LINDA | Oh yes! I think you're going to have fun! |
| SUSAN | Really? I think I'm going to die! |

(LINDA *continues punching and the volume of the music increases as the lights fade. End of Act One.*)

## ACT TWO

*It is a week later.*

*The room is ready for* SUSAN's *fifty-eighth birthday party. The table has been pulled upstage and contains a selection of snacks, etc. There are glasses on the sideboard and birthday cards on display, and some "Happy Birthday" bunting and some balloons hanging above the entrance to the room.* LINDA *enters from the kitchen carrying a bottle of champagne in an ice bucket. She is singing. She places the champagne on the sideboard, moves across to the foot of the stairs, and calls up.*

LINDA   Susan! Are we using napkins?

SUSAN   (*off*) What?

LINDA   Are we using napkins?

SUSAN   (*off*) What?

LINDA   (*yelling*) Are we using bloody napkins?

SUSAN   (*off*) All right, no need to shout. Yes. Right-hand sideboard drawer.

LINDA   Thank you.

(*She heads across, gets a packet of napkins from the drawer and puts them on the table. She then crosses and plumps the cushions on the sofa. Throughout this she has continued to sing, and as she crosses back to the table the singing becomes very enthusiastic.* SUSAN *enters.* LINDA *stops singing when she sees her.* SUSAN *looks truly stunning. Her hair has been styled, she wears full make-up and she is wearing a beautiful, very flattering party dress. It is an amazing transformation.*)

LINDA   My God. You look absolutely stunning.

SUSAN   Thank you kindly.

(*She glides elegantly towards* LINDA.)

LINDA — How wonderful. Come on, give us a twirl.

(SUSAN *gives a twirl and then suddenly stops.*)

SUSAN — Oh, hang on.

(*Her hand goes up under the back of her dress. She starts fiddling in an ungainly fashion, trying to free her underwear from between the cheeks of her bottom.*)

LINDA — How sophisticated. Elegant to uncouth in ten seconds flat.

SUSAN — It's all right for you, but this is very uncomfortable. This over-efficient corsetry contraption has a rather constricting gusset.

(*Her hand goes up under her dress again.*)

LINDA — Well get it sorted out now. We don't want all that in front of the guests.

SUSAN — I thought I wouldn't have to use one of these things. You were supposed to tone me up.

LINDA — You don't get toned-up in a week. These things take time.

SUSAN — So you think it looks all right?

LINDA — When you haven't got your hand stuffed up your bum then yes, it does look all right. In fact, it's more than all right. You look just wonderful.

SUSAN — I don't feel wonderful. It doesn't feel like me.

LINDA — This is the new you. Get used to it.

| | |
|---|---|
| SUSAN | Thank you for doing my hair and make-up, it is extraordinary. I can't believe what I see in the mirror. |
| LINDA | I told you, it's the new you. |
| SUSAN | I just wish this was a bit more comfortable. I won't be able to sit down, you know. |
| LINDA | If we want to look like what we want to look like, comfort has to be sacrificed sometimes. It's a small price to pay. |
| SUSAN | Perhaps I should change this underwear. |
| LINDA | Oh no you don't, this is holding you in nicely. We don't want big bloomers on a night like tonight. |
| SUSAN | I don't always wear big bloomers, excuse me. |
| LINDA | Just forget about your underwear. |
| SUSAN | I wish I could, believe me. I'm reminded of it with every sudden movement I make. I just know I'm going to come unpopped. |
| | (*Her hands go up under the front of the dress, this time as she inspects the poppers.*) |
| LINDA | Don't make sudden movements, then. Retain elegance at all times. |
| SUSAN | Right, I will. |
| LINDA | I have to say, that dress is just . . . well, if I was a man I'd be desperate to get you out of it. |
| SUSAN | Wouldn't do you much good. Thirty seconds to get the dress off, and two hours dismantling the scaffolding. |
| LINDA | Will you stop. I tell you, looking like that, no one's going to call you homely, that's for sure. |

SUSAN  Think so? What would they call me then?

LINDA  Sex on legs, girl. Sex on legs.

SUSAN  I've never thought of myself as that before.

LINDA  You wait till the studs get a sight of you.

SUSAN  Studs? I hardly think they could be classed as studs.

LINDA  They'll turn into studs as soon as they see that dress, don't you worry. I can't wait to see their faces. Oh yes, this is going to be fun. There'll be antlers clashing before the evening's out, you mark my words.

SUSAN  I want no antler-clashing on my birthday, thank you very much. This is the first social occasion for the new selfish me, and I'd like it to go smoothly. (*She crosses to check the table.*)

LINDA  I wonder if there'll be any sex on the agenda?

SUSAN  Linda!

LINDA  It's possible. Looking like you do it's more than possible. And anyway, it won't do you any harm.

SUSAN  Can we change the subject please?

LINDA  Allow yourself to think about it. And you do need to think about it. You need to find yourself a reason.

SUSAN  A reason?

LINDA  Yes. Women need a reason to have sex. Men just need a place.

SUSAN  Well as far as I'm concerned, the only thing on the agenda is my birthday. Oh, I must show

| | |
|---|---|
| | you the present I bought myself. (*She crosses to the sideboard.*) It's a car. |
| LINDA | You bought yourself a car? |
| SUSAN | A Mercedes. (*She crosses back.*) Here we are. (*She shows* LINDA *a model car.*) |
| LINDA | What's this? |
| SUSAN | A model of Richard's car. Well, I'm not sure it's the exact one, but it is a Mercedes. They're all more or less the same aren't they? |
| LINDA | Men don't think so. |
| SUSAN | I know, men and their toys, it's pathetic. A car is a car is a car. As long as it's got four wheels and goes, what's the difference? |
| LINDA | Yes, well . . . if it's not a stupid question, why have you bought yourself a model car? |
| SUSAN | For the voodoo. (*She crosses to the sideboard to collect the pins.*) |
| LINDA | Voodoo? |
| SUSAN | (*crossing back*) Here are the pins. |
| LINDA | You're not serious. |
| SUSAN | Of course I am. Don't know if it'll work or not, but it's worth a try. The perfect birthday present would be if Richard were out with . . . with . . . Lisa . . . (*She spits.*) |
| LINDA | Lisa. (*She spits.*) |
| SUSAN | If they were out somewhere, and they got a flat tyre, that would be a lovely present. Here we go. (*She sticks a pin into one of the tyres.*) I think two, don't you? Then he won't have a |

|||
|---|---|
| | spare. (*She laughs as she sticks in the second pin.*) |
| LINDA | You're mad. |
| SUSAN | No I'm not, this is the sort of thing you do when you're eighteen. |
| LINDA | Eighteen? |
| SUSAN | That's what you told me to do. Think as I did then. Lose the fear you said. Lose the fear, but don't lose the dream. Well, I'm trying to do that, but I also feel as it's my birthday I'm allowed to indulge in a few vengeful thoughts too. |
| | (*The doorbell rings.*) |
| | Oh, here we go. |
| LINDA | I'll get it. |
| | (LINDA *heads for the door.* SUSAN *places the model car and the pins onto the table.*) |
| SUSAN | Oh, hang on. |
| | (LINDA *stops at the door and watches as* SUSAN *fiddles with her bottom again.* SUSAN *stops and straightens her dress.*) |
| LINDA | Finished? |
| SUSAN | Yes, thank you. |
| LINDA | Good. |
| | (LINDA *opens the door and* PETER *steps in.*) |
| PETER | Why didn't you tell me the dog had been sick? |
| LINDA | Nice to see you, too. (*She closes the door.*) |

| | |
|---|---|
| SUSAN | Evening, Peter. |
| PETER | (*he sees her*) Blimey, what have you come as? |
| SUSAN | Oh, thanks very much. |
| LINDA | Don't be so rude. |
| PETER | You could have told me it was fancy-dress. (LINDA *whacks him.*) Happy birthday, Susan. (*He crosses and kisses her on the cheek.*) Well . . . I have to say, you look absolutely edible. You look amazing. You look . . . |
| LINDA | All right, all right, we get the point. No need to dribble. |
| PETER | (*looking at* LINDA) You look all right, too. |
| LINDA | Too late. |
| PETER | (*peering at her closely*) That ointment worked then? (*She whacks him again. He then turns to* SUSAN.) There you go . . . present from us. (*He hands her the gift.*) |
| SUSAN | Ah, thank you. |
| PETER | (*looking at* SUSAN) I can't get over it. Where have you been hiding all these years? I tell you, if I wasn't a married man I'd be chasing you for a date. |
| SUSAN | And I'd tell you that I don't date outside my own species. |
| PETER | Hey, that's not very nice. There was I trying to be kind. |
| LINDA | And if you try getting any kinder you'll get a slap in the face. |

(SUSAN *laughs, and hugs* PETER.)

SUSAN   Oh, Peter, you're lovely. (*She looks at the present.*) Shall I open this now?

LINDA   Whatever.

PETER   No, no, we have to wait for the others.

SUSAN   Oh, okay.

(*The doorbell rings.*)

LINDA   I'll get it. You go and pose somewhere. (*She heads for the door.*)

SUSAN   As long as I don't have to sit. Champagne, Peter?

PETER   I'll get the drinks, you just pose. (*He heads for the drinks.*)

SUSAN   Will everybody stop. I do not pose.

(LINDA *opens the door*, and THOMAS *steps in.*)

LINDA   Hi, Thomas. (*As* THOMAS *closes the door she calls across to* SUSAN.) Greek salad, anyone?

THOMAS  Sorry?

LINDA   Come in, Thomas, come in.

(*She closes the door as* THOMAS *moves into the room.*)

PETER   Evening, Thomas.

THOMAS  Evening, Peter.

SUSAN   Evening, Thomas.

THOMAS  (*he suddenly stops as he sees her*) Eve . . eve . . (LINDA *whacks him on the back.*) . . . evening, Susan. (*He crosses to her.*)

| | |
|---|---|
| SUSAN | You look very smart tonight, Thomas. |
| LINDA | Nice salad dressing. |
| THOMAS | Hap . . . Hap . . . (LINDA *whacks him on the back again.*) . . . Happy birthday. Got a present for you. (*He gives her the present.*) |
| SUSAN | Ah, thank you. |
| THOMAS | For you to open later. |
| SUSAN | Right. |
| THOMAS | You know . . . later. |
| SUSAN | That's what I'm going to do. |
| THOMAS | Good. It's only a silly . . . silly . . . (LINDA *whacks him on the back again.*) No, no, I was all right that time. |
| LINDA | Oh, sorry. |
| THOMAS | Susan, you look fantastic. You look unbelievable. You look . . . |
| LINDA | Another one. All right, all right, we get the point. |
| | (PETER *arrives with two glasses of champagne.*) |
| PETER | There you go, birthday girl. For you, Linda. Champagne, Thomas? |
| THOMAS | Yes please. |
| | (PETER *heads back to the drinks. The doorbell rings.*) |
| LINDA | I'll get it. (*She heads for the door.*) |
| THOMAS | (*to* SUSAN) Have you come to any conclusions? |

| | |
|---|---|
| SUSAN | Conclusions? |
| THOMAS | You know . . . you and me. |
| SUSAN | Not yet, Thomas, I'm still concluding. |

(LINDA *opens the door, and* HENRY *steps in.*)

| | |
|---|---|
| LINDA | Come in, Henry. (*As* HENRY *closes the door she calls across to* SUSAN.) Old Greek God bearing gifts! |
| HENRY | Sorry? |
| LINDA | Nice to see you, Henry. The birthday girl's posing over there. |
| HENRY | Right. (*He turns to greet* SUSAN, *and stops when he sees her, stunned.*) Susan. |
| SUSAN | Evening, Henry. |
| HENRY | Susan. |
| SUSAN | That's me. |
| LINDA | Yes, Henry, that's Susan. |
| HENRY | You look . . . |
| LINDA | Fantastic? |
| HENRY | Yes. |
| LINDA | Stunning? |
| HENRY | Yes. |
| LINDA | Edible? |
| HENRY | Oh yes. |
| LINDA | Right, that's it. I want a dress like that. |

| | |
|---|---|
| HENRY | (*crosses and gives present to* SUSAN) Happy birthday, Susan. |
| SUSAN | Thank you, Henry. |
| | (PETER *approaches with more drinks.*) |
| PETER | Henry, champagne! Thomas. |
| | (*The now all have a drink.*) |
| | Right. A toast. Happy Birthday, Susan. |
| | (*They all chorus* 'happy birthday', *and have a drink.*) |
| | Right. Let's do the usual individual toasts. Make the circle. Susan . . . in the middle. (*They make a circle with* SUSAN *in the middle.*) Okay, who's going first? Henry? |
| HENRY | What? Oh, right, er . . . |
| LINDA | Perhaps he shouldn't go first, he's still in shock from the frock. |
| PETER | All right . . . come on then, Thomas, you go first. |
| THOMAS | Well. As you know I have a passion for mathematics, figures, and statistics. And although you may think it boring, I'm aware that you ladies have a passion for mathematics, too. You divide your age by a third, you double the price of the clothes you buy, and you always add at least five years to the age of your best friends. |
| LINDA | (*to* SUSAN) I sincerely hope you don't. |
| THOMAS | So here's a birthday toast, Susan, to figures and statistics . . . especially yours. To Susan's statistics. |

(*They all toast to 'to* Susan's *statistics'.*)

PETER And that's not easy to say when you've had a few.

LINDA (*to* THOMAS) Well, you're obviously in a saucy mood tonight.

HENRY A bit too saucy for my liking.

PETER Right, your go now, Henry.

HENRY Ah yes, my go. Susan, a toast to you on your birthday. A toast to friendship. 'To the lamp of true friendship. May it burn brightest in our darkest hours, and never flicker in the winds of trial.'

SUSAN Ah, how lovely.

HENRY To friendship.

(*They all toast 'to friendship'.*)

LINDA My go, my go.

PETER Yes all right, go on then.

LINDA To my bestest friend in the whole wide world, here's to the new you. Keep your courage, keep your faith, and keep your dreams. You are truly loved, and here's a toast to . . . the new adventure.

(*They all toast 'the new adventure'.*)

PETER Right, my turn. (*He holds up his glass.*) I drink to your health when I'm with you, I drink to your health when alone, I drink to your health so often, I've just about wrecked my own! (*He does a mock drunken stagger.*)

| | |
|---|---|
| SUSAN | Oh, thank you everyone. I'm just so lucky to have such lovely friends. (*She raises her glass.*) To you! |
| | (*They all toast 'to us'.*) |
| LINDA | Presents, presents! |
| SUSAN | Oh yes, presents. |
| THOMAS | You're doing them now? I thought you said later. |
| SUSAN | This is later. |
| THOMAS | No, no, I meant . . . |
| LINDA | No, come on Thomas, she has to do it now. |
| SUSAN | Right. Which one first? (*She picks up one of the presents from the table.*) |
| THOMAS | I'll just er . . . (*He picks up his present and turns to* PETER.) I'll give it to her later. It's only a silly thing . . . you know, gloves and scarf . . . just to keep her warm . . . silly really. |
| | (SUSAN *seems to be taking a long time opening the present.*) |
| LINDA | Come on, come on! |
| SUSAN | All right, all right, don't get your knickers in a twist. |
| LINDA | As long as you don't get yours in a twist again, that's all I'm worried about. |
| | (*The present is now open. It is a book.*) |
| SUSAN | Love Poems by John Donne. Oh, thank you, Henry. (*She crosses and kisses him on the cheek.*) How lovely. (*She crosses back to the table.*) |

| | |
|---|---|
| PETER | (*sidling up to him*) Love poems eh, Henry? |
| HENRY | No, no, I just . . . they're lovely poems. |
| PETER | You old rascal. |
| HENRY | No, no . . . |
| SUSAN | (*opening another present*) From Linda and Peter . . . oh, two presents. (*The first one is a CD.*) "Hits of the Sixties" – Oh, wonderful. (*She kisses* LINDA *on the cheek.*) |
| LINDA | Stuff to strut your stuff to. |
| | (*She opens the second one. It is a china ornament of two birds sitting on a branch.*) |
| SUSAN | Oh . . . for my collection. Thank you so much. (*She kisses* PETER *on the cheek.*) How clever of you to choose that. |
| PETER | Yes, it's nice to know what I bought you. |
| LINDA | (*whacking him*) I told you what it was. |
| PETER | No you didn't. |
| LINDA | You don't listen. He never listens. He's the world's expert at selective deafness. |
| PETER | Excuse me, but I certainly wouldn't have gone out and bought her two tits on a trunk! |
| SUSAN | Now, now, let's not have a domestic, not this evening. |
| LINDA | Yours now, Thomas. |
| THOMAS | Oh . . . er . . . no, it's just silly. Open it later. |
| SUSAN | Of course it won't be silly. |

| | |
|---|---|
| LINDA | Come on. |
| THOMAS | No, really... |
| LINDA | It's the thought that counts. At least you bought something yourself. (*She turns to* PETER.) Which is more than he did. Come on Thomas, we want to get on to the drinking and dancing. |
| THOMAS | Look, I really think you should wait till later. |
| SUSAN | Oh come on, Thomas, let me see. |

(SUSAN *goes to take the present.* THOMAS *doesn't want to let go of it. There is a subtle tug-of-war, and eventually* SUSAN *gets it from him.*)

| | |
|---|---|
| THOMAS | Susan! |
| SUSAN | Will you stop. I'm sure it'll be lovely. |

(*She opens the present and pulls out a sexy red pair of lacy, very brief knickers.*)

Oh.

(HENRY *splutters on his drink.*)

| | |
|---|---|
| PETER | Well they'll certainly keep her warm all right, Thomas. |

(SUSAN *then pulls out a matching lacy red bra and a suspender belt.*)

| | |
|---|---|
| SUSAN | Well. Thank you, Thomas. That's er... that's just what I need. |
| PETER | So, Thomas, how did you know what size to get? |
| HENRY | (*glaring at* THOMAS) Yes, I'd like to know that, too. |

| | |
|---|---|
| THOMAS | Oh, well . . . I just thought . . . |
| SUSAN | Thank you, Thomas, this is just perfect for the new me. (*She kisses him on the cheek.* HENRY *continues to glare at him.*) Thank you everyone for my lovely presents. And now . . . some more drinks! |
| PETER | Yes indeed, more drinks! Champagne for everyone! (*He gets the bottle and starts topping-up everyone's glasses.*) |
| LINDA | And music. We need music. I'll put the new CD on. (*She heads across to put the music on.*) |
| PETER | (*to* THOMAS *as he tops up his glass*) I don't know if you should have any more, Thomas. You're in a dangerous mood tonight. |
| THOMAS | No, no, I just . . . |
| HENRY | Well I was a bit shocked, I must say. Rather personal, that present. |
| THOMAS | It was meant to be personal. |
| HENRY | Bit too personal, if you ask me. |

(*The music starts. The track is "Will You Still Love Me Tomorrow", by the Shirelles.*)

| | |
|---|---|
| SUSAN | Oh I love this. Who's for the first dance? Henry? |
| HENRY | Oh, er . . . I haven't done this for a very long time. |
| SUSAN | No time like the present. |
| HENRY | Well . . . er . . . |
| THOMAS | I'll dance with you. |
| HENRY | (*quickly*) It's all right. She asked me first! |

(*He quickly grabs hold of* SUSAN, *and they start to dance.*)

LINDA  Come on, Thomas, I'm available.

THOMAS  Oh, right. Doesn't Peter want to?

LINDA  No, he's better on his own. Less dangerous.

(LINDA *and* THOMAS *start to dance.* PETER *dances on his own.* LINDA *and* THOMAS *manoeuvre away, and are replaced centre-stage by* SUSAN *and* HENRY.)

HENRY  I wondered if you'd had any more thoughts?

SUSAN  Thoughts?

HENRY  About what I said the other day.

SUSAN  I'm still thinking, Henry.

HENRY  Because I meant what I said.

SUSAN  I know you did.

HENRY  You're lovely.

SUSAN  Well I've scrubbed up well tonight.

HENRY  You're beautiful . . . even without that dress. Oh no, I didn't mean . . . what I meant was . . . oh, God . . .

(*They manoeuvre away and are replaced centre-stage by* THOMAS *and* LINDA.)

THOMAS  It was so embarrassing. I didn't want anyone else to see.

LINDA  For your eyes only, eh? You little tinker, you.

THOMAS  No, no, I just meant . . .

LINDA  Don't worry, Thomas, we all know what you meant. And I thought it was a wonderful present... a wonderful first move. Now, would you like some advice about what to do next?

THOMAS  Next?

LINDA  Auntie Linda will tell you exactly what to do.

(*They manoeuvre away as* PETER *replaces them, enthusiastically dancing on his own and singing along to the song. He manoeuvres away and is replaced centre-stage by* SUSAN *and* HENRY.)

HENRY  I'm glad you liked the book.

SUSAN  It's lovely, Henry.

HENRY  Sorry I didn't get you any underpants.

SUSAN  Underpants? No, no, that's fine. And if that's how you class them, perhaps it's better that you didn't get me any.

HENRY  Sorry?

SUSAN  The book is perfect.

HENRY  Not that I don't think of you in that way.

SUSAN  What way's that, Henry?

HENRY  You know... in er...

(LINDA *moves across and fades out the music.*)

SUSAN  (*in the silence*) In underpants?

(HENRY *splutters. The others register* SUSAN's *remark.*)

LINDA  Right. Time for something a bit livelier.

(*She starts the track of Chuck Berry singing "Johnny B Goode".*)

| SUSAN | Oh yes. Come on, Henry, let's go for it. You used to be good at this. |
|---|---|
| HENRY | I've forgotten how. |
| SUSAN | No you haven't. Turn it up, Linda. |
| | (LINDA *turns up the volume.*) |
| LINDA | (*to* SUSAN) Come on, girl, give us a twirl. |
| | (SUSAN *twirls as* LINDA *heads across to* THOMAS.) |
| | Come on, Thomas, I'll teach you to jive. |
| | (SUSAN *applauds as* LINDA *and* THOMAS *attempt a jive. She then heads across to* HENRY, *grabs him, and he reluctantly starts to jive.* LINDA *and* THOMAS *are enthusiastically jigging together, and* PETER *gets more lively on his own. It takes a while for* HENRY *to warm up, but then they go for it. A full-bodied jive, with all the expansive movements, etc. They seem transported back to their youth, are both very good at the jive, and once they've got going the others watch the featured dance, clapping along, laughing, cheering and jigging on the spot, etc. At the end of the dance, they all applaud and cheer.*) |
| SUSAN | Oh, Henry, that was great. |
| HENRY | (*wheezing as he crawls on all fours to the sofa*) Oh, my God. I haven't done that for twenty-five years. And the way I'm feeling now, it'll be another twenty-five years before I do it again. |
| SUSAN | Slow track now please, Linda. |
| LINDA | I think that's best. (*She heads to the CD player.*) |

| | |
|---|---|
| HENRY | Just let me get my breath back. |
| | (THOMAS *approaches* SUSAN. *He is very surly.*) |
| THOMAS | (*surly*) This is my dance, I think. |
| SUSAN | Oh. Certainly, young sir. |
| HENRY | No, no, I'll be all right in a minute. |
| THOMAS | (*very firmly*) This is my dance, I said! |
| HENRY | Fair enough. |
| | (*The music starts. The track is "I Say A Little Prayer" by Aretha Franklin.* THOMAS *and* SUSAN *manoeuvre centre-stage.* LINDA *and* PETER *start dancing behind them.*) |
| THOMAS | (*very surly*) Hope you liked the present. |
| | (SUSAN *looks at him quizzically.*) |
| SUSAN | Yes. Yes I did. Bit of a surprise, I must say. |
| THOMAS | (*still surly*) Nice, I hope. |
| SUSAN | Yes, it was a nice surprise. I haven't been bought underwear for about thirty years. |
| THOMAS | You've been wearing thirty-year-old underwear? |
| SUSAN | Thomas! |
| | (*They manoeuvre away and are replaced centre-stage by* LINDA *and* PETER.) |
| LINDA | Mind my feet. Mind my feet! |
| PETER | Don't keep getting them in the way then. Here, did you hear about the parachutist who jumped |

|         | out of the plane and then his parachute wouldn't open? |
|---|---|
| LINDA | Oh no, don't start on the jokes, please. |
| PETER | He was plummeting to earth desperately trying to find the emergency ripcord, when he suddenly sees this bloke plummeting up. So he yells to this bloke, "Do you know anything about parachutes?" And the other yells, "No. Do you know anything about gas cookers?" |
| LINDA | Oh, God. |

(*They manoeuvre away and are replaced centre-stage by* SUSAN *and* THOMAS.)

| THOMAS | (*still surly*) So you'll let me know, then, will you? |
|---|---|
| SUSAN | Let you know about what? |
| THOMAS | (*still surly*) Your new underwear. |
| SUSAN | What about it? |
| THOMAS | (*still surly*) You know . . . when you want me to see if it fits all right. |
| SUSAN | If it fits all right? |

(HENRY *approaches them.*)

| HENRY | Excuse me, but is this an 'excuse me'? |
|---|---|
| THOMAS | (*very surly*) Excuse me, but it's not! |

(*They brush past* HENRY, *still remaining central.*
HENRY, *very disgruntled, moves back to the sofa.*)

| SUSAN | Thomas, are you all right? |

| | |
|---|---|
| THOMAS | (*still surly*) What do you mean? |
| SUSAN | You seem a bit . . . angry. |
| THOMAS | Oh, I know, I'm sorry. I wasn't trying to be angry, as such. I was just doing what Linda said. |
| SUSAN | What Linda said? |
| THOMAS | Well, she said that as I'd made such a good start with the present, I ought to keep it going. So she was giving me some toy boy advice. |
| SUSAN | Toy boy advice? |
| THOMAS | She said I should try being mean and moody. She said that's what toy boys do. What do you think? |
| SUSAN | I think you just look constipated. |
| THOMAS | Oh, right. That's probably because she also told me to clench my buttocks a lot. Tighten up, you know. I don't know if you noticed? |
| SUSAN | Not yet, but I'll keep an eye out for it. |

(HENRY *approaches again.*)

| | |
|---|---|
| HENRY | Excuse me, but I don't think you're allowed to refuse an 'excuse me' if someone wants an 'excuse me'. So excuse me. |

(HENRY *tries to take over, but* THOMAS *resists.*)

| | |
|---|---|
| THOMAS | (*very firmly*) Excuse me, this is my dance, excuse me! |
| LINDA | No fighting boys, I'm still here. And I'm desperate for rescue. |

(*The doorbell rings.*)

|   |   |
|---|---|
|  | Ah hah! Saved by the bell. I'll get it. (*She heads for the door.*) |
| HENRY | Susan, tell him. Dance floor etiquette requires that you should never refuse an 'excuse me.' |
| THOMAS | Excuse me, but why can't you wait for the next dance, excuse me. |
| HENRY | Because an 'excuse me' means you don't have to wait for the next one, excuse me! |
|  | (LINDA *opens the door.* RICHARD, SUSAN'S *husband, steps in.*) |
| LINDA | Richard. |
| RICHARD | Linda. (*He then sees the gathering.*) Oh. |
|  | (SUSAN *then sees him. She is obviously very surprised.*) |
| SUSAN | Richard. |
| RICHARD | Sorry. I didn't realise you were having a party. |
| SUSAN | It's my birthday. |
| RICHARD | I know. That's why I'm here. I've bought you a present. |
| SUSAN | Oh. |
|  | (*There is a slightly awkward moment.* RICHARD *then turns and greets* PETER.) |
| RICHARD | Peter. |
| PETER | Hi, Richard. How's it hanging? |
| RICHARD | (*greeting the others*) Henry. Thomas. (*He turns to* SUSAN.) Look, I'm sorry, I didn't mean to intrude. |

| | |
|---|---|
| SUSAN | You are intruding. |
| RICHARD | (*he crosses to her*) Could I just have five minutes, please? |
| SUSAN | Turn the music off please, Thomas. |
| | (THOMAS *goes and turns the music off.*) |
| RICHARD | Sorry, I didn't mean to ruin the atmosphere. |
| SUSAN | You just did. Okay. Let's get it over with, get you out of here, and then we can get on. |
| RICHARD | I just needed to speak to you. |
| SUSAN | Ever heard of a telephone? |
| LINDA | Excuse me, do I shut this door or what? |
| | (SUSAN *just shrugs, and* LINDA *closes the door.*) |
| RICHARD | I needed to speak to you in person. |
| SUSAN | We can talk tomorrow. |
| RICHARD | This is important, Susan. |
| SUSAN | So am I, Richard, so am I. In fact, I am very important. The new me is never going to be unimportant ever again. Like the new me? |
| RICHARD | You look wonderful. |
| SUSAN | How's Lisa? |
| | (LINDA *spits. They all turn and look at her.*) |
| LINDA | Sorry, I'm so sorry. It was an automatic response. |
| RICHARD | (*to* SUSAN) I'm not here to talk about Lisa. |
| | (LINDA *spits again. Again they all look at her.*) |

| | |
|---|---|
| LINDA | Sorry, sorry! That will not happen again. |
| SUSAN | So, what did you want to talk about? |
| RICHARD | Could we go into the other room? |
| SUSAN | I'm fine here, thank you. |
| RICHARD | I just need five minutes, please. |
| SUSAN | You won't need that much to upset me, surely. Okay, go ahead. |
| RICHARD | Susan, this is important. |
| SUSAN | So you said. |

(*He looks at her for a moment, and then turns to the others.*)

RICHARD  I'm sorry, I'm really sorry for this interruption, but I have something private I'd like to say to Susan. Would you please excuse us?

(*The others all start to move.*)

SUSAN  Nobody move!

(*They all stop.* SUSAN *turns to* RICHARD.)

If you have something to say, it can be said in front of them. These are my loyal friends. Remember loyal?

RICHARD  Susan, please . . .

HENRY  It's all right, Susan, we'll just wait in the other room (*He turns to the others.*) Come on.

(*They start to move.*)

SUSAN  Nobody move, I said!

(*They all stop again.*)

I want you here.

PETER
Susan, it's all right. Have your five minutes. We'll be fine in there.

HENRY
Yes, don't worry about us.

(HENRY, THOMAS, *and* PETER *head into the kitchen.* LINDA *doesn't move.* PETER *stops at the door and turns to her.*)

PETER
Linda?

LINDA
You carry on, I'm okay here for a minute.

PETER
Linda.

LINDA
I won't be in the way.

PETER
Linda!

(*She sulkily follows him into the kitchen.*)

SUSAN
Well. How to ruin a party in sixty seconds flat. Go on then, you've got five minutes. (*She looks at her watch.*) Come on, time's running out.

(*He just looks at her for a moment.*)

RICHARD
Susan. I want to come back.

SUSAN
What?

RICHARD
Here. With you.

SUSAN
You want to come back?

RICHARD
I've made a terrible mistake. I'm sorry. Please . . . I want to come back.

(*We see she is totally thrown.*)

| | |
|---|---|
| SUSAN | Richard, you . . . you can't come here, like this, and . . . and just say that . . . like that. |
| RICHARD | I don't know how else to say it. |
| SUSAN | But it's my birthday. I don't want this on my birthday. |
| RICHARD | I'm sorry. But I didn't want to do this on the telephone. I wasn't sure if you'd be doing anything this evening, and anyway, I had intended to be here much earlier . . . but I got a flat tyre. |
| SUSAN | (*she stops*) You got a flat tyre? |
| RICHARD | Brand new tyre. Can't understand it. |
| SUSAN | Me neither. Only the one was it? |
| RICHARD | Sorry? |
| SUSAN | Oh, nothing, nothing. |
| RICHARD | Susan, I've been such an idiot. |
| SUSAN | Yes, you have. |
| RICHARD | And I am so sorry. |
| SUSAN | (*she looks at him*) But you . . . you wanted a divorce. |
| RICHARD | That's not going to happen now. |
| SUSAN | But you got that far in your mind, Richard. I mean, moving out's one thing . . . |
| RICHARD | It was all a mistake, a madness. I don't want a divorce now. |
| SUSAN | What if I want a divorce? |

RICHARD (*he stops*) Do you?

(*She looks at him for a moment.*)

SUSAN So what's gone wrong, then? What's happened to love's young dream?

RICHARD I've told you . . . it was all a mistake.

SUSAN You told me you loved her.

RICHARD I thought I did . . . but I obviously didn't.

SUSAN You didn't love her? So this has all been about a bit on the side has it? A bit on the side that got a bit out of hand, is that what you're saying? So come on, tell me what happened.

RICHARD It's just . . . it's just not right. I've been living a lie these past few months, trying to make something work, that I knew in my heart could never work. I just thought . . . stupidly . . . that I needed something in my life . . . something . . .

SUSAN Less boring?

RICHARD No.

SUSAN Less frumpy and dumpy?

RICHARD No.

SUSAN Less homely?

RICHARD No. Susan, listen to me. I love you. I still love you.

SUSAN Really? You've got an interesting way of showing it.

RICHARD I want to try and start repairing. I'd like us to talk. I realise this evening is not the most appropriate time, but I needed to see you. I'd

|        | like another chance, Susan. Will you think about it? |
|--------|---|
| SUSAN | Of course I'll think about it, I've done nothing but think about it. (*She stops.*) Does she know you're here? |
| RICHARD | No. No, she doesn't. |
| SUSAN | Does she know you want to finish it? |
| RICHARD | No. Not yet. |
| SUSAN | Waiting to see what I'll say first. |
| RICHARD | No, it's not that. Susan, I was rather pushed into asking you for a divorce . . . weak of me I know . . . but ever since then I've realised how much I miss you. I know I've hurt you, and I am so sorry. You're the one person on this earth I shouldn't hurt. Please, Susan . . . I'd like another chance. |
| SUSAN | It's not that easy Richard . . . there are so many things . . . |
| RICHARD | And we'll talk about those things. I just know that we should be with each other. We've had most of our lives together, we know each other so well . . . |
| SUSAN | I thought I knew you. |
| RICHARD | . . . and if I could turn the clock back . . . |
| SUSAN | Yes, well we'd all like that. I'd like to turn the clock back and be eighteen again. Wouldn't make the same mistakes next time round. No marriage for you and me, that's for sure. |
| RICHARD | Please don't dismiss our marriage. |
| SUSAN | Why not? That's what you've been trying to do. |

| | |
|---|---|
| RICHARD | (*he looks at her*) Susan, I miss you so much. I'm such an idiot, and I really wish . . . I really wish this had never happened. |
| SUSAN | So do I, Richard, so do I. |
| RICHARD | Susan. I promise . . . |
| SUSAN | Oh, don't make promises, Richard, please. (*She looks at him.*) Do you have any idea how angry and disappointed I am with you? |
| RICHARD | Susan, I know what a wonderful person you are, and I know there have been times when I've taken you for granted . . . but I know now that I don't want to be with anyone else. |
| SUSAN | So why did you lose sight of me then? |
| RICHARD | I didn't lose sight of you . . . not in my heart . . . I just . . . I just had a madness on me. I don't know how else to describe it. All I know is, I now feel so ashamed . . . and devastated at the thought that I might have lost you forever. Please don't hate me. |
| SUSAN | Of course I don't hate you. I'd like to stick your head in a winepress, but I don't hate you. |
| RICHARD | What is this with the winepress? |
| SUSAN | I don't know. And don't get picky. If I could think of a better alternative I would. (*She crosses and sits on the sofa. As she sits she reacts to the discomfort of her underwear.*) |
| RICHARD | Do you . . . do you miss me at all? |
| SUSAN | About as much as I'd miss haemorrhoids. |
| RICHARD | Seriously. |

| | |
|---|---|
| SUSAN | (*she looks at him*) Yes. Yes, I do miss you. And there are times when it is so unbearable, I don't know what to do with myself. I don't want to be on my own . . . the thought of it is just so daunting . . . |
| RICHARD | (*he crosses and sits on the sofa next to her*) Please, Susan, it was just a mistake . . . a stupid, stupid mistake. |
| SUSAN | But how did it happen? That's what I don't understand. I thought we'd passed the point for a mid-life crisis. I mean, you're not mid any more, you're mid to late . . . and that's being kind. I thought you were a grown-up person. Huh. Too much to hope for there, I suppose. Grown-up males these days are an endangered species. (*She looks at him.*) God, what an idiot you've been. |
| RICHARD | I don't want to lose you, Susan, and I want you to try to forgive me. |
| SUSAN | Oh, Richard . . . |
| | (*Suddenly,* THOMAS *bursts through the kitchen doorway, closely followed by the others.*) |
| THOMAS | Don't do it, Susan. Don't do it! |
| LINDA | Thomas. Thomas! |
| THOMAS | You don't have to do it Susan. You don't have to do it! |
| SUSAN | (*rising*) Thomas, please . . . |
| RICHARD | (*rising*) What the hell is going on here? |
| THOMAS | Before you say anything to him, remember my offer! |
| LINDA | (*trying to restrain him*) Thomas! |

| | |
|---|---|
| RICHARD | Have you been listening to us? How dare you. |
| SUSAN | (*she crosses to him*) Thomas, please go back into the kitchen. Linda, take him back. |
| LINDA | Come on, Thomas. (*She grabs him.*) |
| THOMAS | (*freeing himself*) No, I will not be quietened. I want my say. (*He turns on* RICHARD.) How dare I? How dare you, you mean. You haven't seen how much she's cried. You haven't seen her total despair. Well we have. And we're her friends, and we don't like it, and it's all your fault, and I personally am not going to let it happen again. |
| SUSAN | Thomas, please . . . |
| RICHARD | This is private business. This is nothing to do with you. |
| SUSAN | Please, Thomas, this is not the time. |
| THOMAS | It is exactly the time. (*He turns to* RICHARD.) And it most certainly is to do with me, because I'm now part of Susan's choice. I'm on offer. |
| RICHARD | Offer? What the hell are you talking about? |
| | (THOMAS *grabs the lacy red knickers from the table.*) |
| THOMAS | This. This is what I'm talking about. This is what I'm offering. (*He waves the knickers at* RICHARD.) When was the last time you bought anything like this? |
| RICHARD | Has he gone stark, staring mad? |
| THOMAS | No more will she have to wear thirty-year-old underwear. |
| SUSAN | Thomas! |

| | |
|---|---|
| THOMAS | She deserves better. |
| LINDA | I should think she does. |
| THOMAS | (*he waves the knickers at* RICHARD) This is what she deserves. (*He turns and waves the knickers at* SUSAN.) This is what you deserve, Susan. And this is what you're going to have. |
| SUSAN | Will you please stop waving my knickers in the air! (*She snatches them away from him.*) |
| THOMAS | Please, Susan, you must think carefully. |
| SUSAN | Thomas, you have got to stop this. |
| RICHARD | (*to* THOMAS) How dare you! How dare you interrupt a private conversation between me and my wife. Who the hell do you think you are? |
| THOMAS | Who the hell do I think I am? I'll tell you who the hell I think I am. I'm Thomas the toy boy! |
| SUSAN | Thomas! |
| LINDA | Peter. Do something! |
| PETER | I am doing something. I'm waiting to see what he's going to do next. (LINDA *whacks him.*) |
| RICHARD | Toy boy? (*He turns to* SUSAN.) Toy boy? You don't mean . . . you and this . . . this . . . stick insect? |
| THOMAS | And what about you and that . . . that . . . (*He spits.*) . . . whatsername? |
| RICHARD | Susan, you can't be serious. |
| THOMAS | Oh this is serious, all right. And I'll tell you how serious it is. I've never clenched my buttocks for anyone before tonight. |

| | |
|---|---|
| RICHARD | What? |
| THOMAS | But I've clenched for Susan. And now that I'm being trained-up to be mean and moody . . . |
| RICHARD | He's mad. He's totally mad. |
| SUSAN | Thomas, that's enough, do you hear me? Now go back into the dining room. I'm quite capable of dealing with this myself. |
| THOMAS | I'm not leaving you alone with that . . . that . . . dog mess! |
| RICHARD | Dog mess? |
| SUSAN | Thomas, please . . . |
| RICHARD | Right, that's it. I've had enough of this. (*He turns on* THOMAS.) I want you out of this house now. |
| SUSAN | Richard! |
| RICHARD | I will not accept this appalling behaviour. (*To* THOMAS.) And if you don't leave right now, I'll throw you out myself. |
| THOMAS | Oh yeah, you and whose army? |
| SUSAN | (*to* RICHARD) Just a minute, you can't throw him out of this house. |
| RICHARD | (*to* THOMAS) Go on, get out! |
| THOMAS | You couldn't throw me out of anywhere. |
| SUSAN | He is my guest. This is my house. You most certainly will not throw him out. |
| THOMAS | Go and get . . . (*He spits.*) . . . whatsername to help you. Then you might have a chance. |
| RICHARD | How dare you talk to me like that. |

| | |
|---|---|
| SUSAN | Are you listening to me Richard? I will not have this. This is my house. |
| THOMAS | (*to* RICHARD) You're the one that should get out. Go on, get out! |
| SUSAN | Stop it, Thomas! |
| RICHARD | Right. That is it. |

(*He goes to grab* THOMAS.)

Get out!

(*Suddenly*, HENRY *rushes in between* RICHARD *and* THOMAS.)

| | |
|---|---|
| HENRY | Stop this. Stop this now! Do you hear me? That is enough! Now calm down, calm right down! |

(*They all stop.*)

This is Susan's birthday. I will not have this behaviour.

| | |
|---|---|
| THOMAS | It's his fault! |
| RICHARD | It's your fault! |
| HENRY | Stop it! Stop it, the pair of you. I don't care whose fault it is, I want no more of it. Just think about Susan for a minute. |
| RICHARD | I am thinking about Susan, that's why I'm here. I'm her husband. (*He points at* THOMAS.) He's the one. He has no right to . . . |
| THOMAS | I have rights. I have toy boy rights. Right Linda? |
| LINDA | Thomas . . . |

| | |
|---|---|
| THOMAS | (*to* SUSAN) He may be your husband Susan, but that doesn't give him the right to treat you the way he did. You've got a choice now, remember that . . . you don't have to get back with him. |
| RICHARD | Choice? You call yourself a choice? |
| THOMAS | Yes I do. And I'm a choice choice! |
| HENRY | All right, all right, that's enough! (*They stop.*) Your behaviour is absolutely disgraceful. It's common sense and calm we need here, not aggression. The solution to all this is quite simple. We just need to be grown-up about it, that's all. And that is exactly what I am going to be. (*He turns to* SUSAN.) Susan. (*He then suddenly gets on one knee.*) Marry me? |

(*The others all stop, totally stunned.*)

| | |
|---|---|
| SUSAN | Henry. |
| PETER | And this is grown-up? |
| HENRY | Susan, I love you with all my heart, and I always have done. I'll divorce Elizabeth, and I'll look after you, I'll be loyal to you, and I will love you till the day I die. Please Susan . . . marry me. |
| LINDA | Tomorrow I definitely buy a dress like that. |
| SUSAN | Henry, get up please. |
| HENRY | (*struggling up*) Easier said than done. |
| RICHARD | What the hell do you think you're playing at Henry? I thought you were my friend. |
| HENRY | I am your friend. That's why I didn't do this twenty-five years ago. |
| SUSAN | Henry, please, this is not the time. |

| | |
|---|---|
| THOMAS | That's right. Talk of marriage at this time is very inappropriate. She's already done that once, and look where it's got her. She needs a short-term solution . . . and I am that solution. |
| HENRY | Yes, well I'm talking about love here, not lust. |
| THOMAS | A bit of lust is what she could do with right now. |
| SUSAN | Excuse me, it most certainly is not! |
| LINDA | Well I wouldn't mind a bit of lust. Oh, sorry. |
| PETER | Linda! |
| LINDA | (*sees* PETER'S *startled look*) Don't worry, I didn't mean with you. |
| RICHARD | (*to* HENRY) What do you mean, twenty-five years ago? What the hell happened between you two twenty-five years ago? |
| HENRY | Nowhere near enough, that's what happened. |
| SUSAN | Excuse me, can I say something here? This is my birthday. I just wanted to enjoy myself. Today is supposed to be about me . . . the new me . . . not about you three. |
| HENRY | I'm sorry, Susan. I didn't mean this to happen tonight, but they made me. |
| THOMAS | What do you mean, we made you? |
| RICHARD | Made you? No one made you get on your knee Henry. (*He turns on* THOMAS.) And you keep out of this! |
| | (RICHARD *and* THOMAS *continue to argue loudly.* SUSAN *tries to speak. Eventually she just yells.*) |
| SUSAN | (*yelling*) Let me speak! |

(*They all stop.*)

Now sit down, the three of you. Go on Richard, sit down! Sit!

(RICHARD *sits in the armchair*, HENRY *and* THOMAS *sit on the sofa.*)

Well, I certainly hadn't intended to deal with all this on my birthday. But now that things have got so out of hand, it looks as though I'll have to. I can't believe what's happening here tonight. I haven't had as much male attention since my buttons popped open at the Cricket Club prizegiving. (*To* RICHARD.) You want me to take you back. (*To* HENRY.) You want to marry me. (*To* THOMAS.) And you want some lacy red lambada.

LINDA  Oh, that's a good one.

SUSAN  Thank you. (*She looks at the three men.*) God, what a choice.

RICHARD  Choice? What do you mean choice? I'm not staying here to be part of some stupid competition.

THOMAS  Leave then.

HENRY  Yes, go on, leave, there's the door.

RICHARD  Don't talk to me like that!

SUSAN  All right, all right!

(*They stop, and she turns to* THOMAS.)

Dear Thomas. I am very flattered and, I have to admit, a mite flustered by your extraordinary offer. Your suggestions have certainly made me twitter a bit, and that's something I haven't experienced for a very long time. (*She turns to*

|         | HENRY.) Henry. I don't know what to say. Your proposition has left me quite speechless. You said some wonderful things. I do feel truly loved . . . and that's wonderful . . . and it's only fair that I don't string any of you along. I don't want either of you to be upset, but my choice is quite simple really. In fact, it's the only choice I could make under the circumstances. Richard . . . I choose me! (*She makes a grand extravagant gesture, with her arms in the air.*) Me! |
|---------|---|
| LINDA   | Yes. Oh yes! |
|         | (SUSAN *crosses and embraces* LINDA. *She then turns, and crosses to* RICHARD.) |
| SUSAN   | Richard, 39 years is a very long time . . . and they do say that everyone's allowed one mistake along the way. Of course I can forgive you, but this is about me. Me. Do you understand? I've never been truly selfish in my life before, and I'd like to see where that leads me. I don't want to go back, I want to go forward, and if I feel I'd like to go forward with you . . . you'll be the first to know.<br>(*She turns to* THOMAS.) Thomas, I thank you with all my heart. It's nicely surprising at my age to be lusted after so fervently. I don't know if I would ever go down that toy boy route, but if I do . . . you'll be the first to know.<br>(*She turns to* HENRY.) Henry, you were romantic, moving, and sincere, and you touched my heart. I don't know if I would ever want to get married again, but if I do . . . you'll be the first to know.<br>(*She stops and looks at the three of them.*) Please don't be downhearted . . . I haven't said no to any of you. |
| LINDA   | Er, excuse me, Susan. I'm not sure you should burn all your bridges like this. |
| SUSAN   | Sorry? |

| | |
|---|---|
| LINDA | While they're all so keen, why not give each of them a trial period? |
| SUSAN | Trial period? |
| LINDA | Remember that rota system we talked about? The first week of the month have him . . . (*She points at* THOMAS.) . . . second week him . . . (*She points at* HENRY.) . . . third week him . . . (*She points at* RICHARD.) . . . and in the fourth week you can rest a bit and catch up with the personal training. |
| SUSAN | Well . . . |
| PETER | (*rising*) Excuse me. That fourth week. Instead of . . . |
| LINDA | Don't even think about it! (PETER *sits back down.*) |
| SUSAN | Thank you, Linda, that is a very interesting and a very colourful suggestion. |
| RICHARD | (*rising*) Oh this is just ridiculous! I'm not listening to any more of this. How dare you put me alongside these morons. |
| THOMAS | Just because she didn't choose you. |
| HENRY | And I noticed you stayed to see what the outcome would be. Why didn't you leave earlier if it bothered you that much? |
| RICHARD | Because I'm a bigger fool than I thought I was. (*He heads for the door.*) |
| SUSAN | (*following him*) Richard, please don't be upset. |
| RICHARD | (*he stops*) Don't be upset? I'm your husband. I deserve better than this. I came here this evening to try and save our marriage. I didn't |

|         | expect to find myself in the middle of a childish farce. |
|---------|---|
| SUSAN   | I didn't expect it either. |
| RICHARD | Well at least you've made your position quite clear. (*He opens the door.*) |
| SUSAN   | Richard, if you do need to talk . . . |
| RICHARD | Goodbye. (*He leaves.*) |
| SUSAN   | . . . I'd be happy to talk. (*The door closes.*) Bye.<br><br>(*She turns back into the room.*) |
| THOMAS  | Susan, I'm so sorry. This is my fault. I shouldn't have started all that. |
| SUSAN   | It's all right, Thomas, please don't worry. (*She pulls herself together.*) Right. Enough is enough! This is my birthday. I want jollity and enjoyment . . . and another drink please. |
| PETER   | Coming right up. (*He gets the bottle and starts topping-up their glasses.*) |
| SUSAN   | And I'll tell you what else I want. (*She turns to* THOMAS *and* HENRY.) I want no more long faces from you two. It's my birthday! |
| PETER   | It's her birthday! Come on, get your glasses.<br><br>(SUSAN *encourages* HENRY *and* THOMAS *to get up.*) |
| SUSAN   | Yes, more champagne! |
| PETER   | A toast! Come on, come on. (*They all now have their drinks.*) Well done this evening, birthday girl. That was some performance. (*He raises his glass.*) To the new independent Susan! |

*(They all toast 'the new independent Susan'.)*

SUSAN  Linda!

LINDA  What?

SUSAN  Where's the music?

LINDA  *(she heads for the music)* Running all the way, running all the way.

SUSAN  Come on, Henry, dance with me. Fast track please, Linda!

HENRY  No, please, not a fast one.

*(The Chuck Berry track, 'Johnny B Goode' starts.)*

Oh, no.

SUSAN  Oh, yes. *(She grabs him.)* Here we go, Henry. *(They start to jive.)*

LINDA  Come on, Thomas. *(She grabs THOMAS, and they start to jive.* PETER *jigs on his own again.)*

*(The doorbell rings.)*

PETER  Doorbell. Doorbell! *(He heads for the door.)*

SUSAN  Oh, what now?

LINDA  *(turning the music down)* Mean and moody young Greek God please!

*(PETER opens the door and RICHARD steps in.)*

PETER  Richard.

RICHARD  Sorry. I haven't got my mobile with me. I need to use the phone please.

SUSAN  Help yourself.

| | |
|---|---|
| RICHARD | Thank you. (*He heads for the phone.*) I just don't bloody understand it. I've got another flat tyre! |
| SUSAN | (*punching the air*) Yes. Oh, yes! Turn the music up! |
| | (LINDA *turns the music up.*) |
| RICHARD | (*dialling*) Turn that music down! |
| | (*They all start enthusiastically jiving. The lights fade. The end.*) |

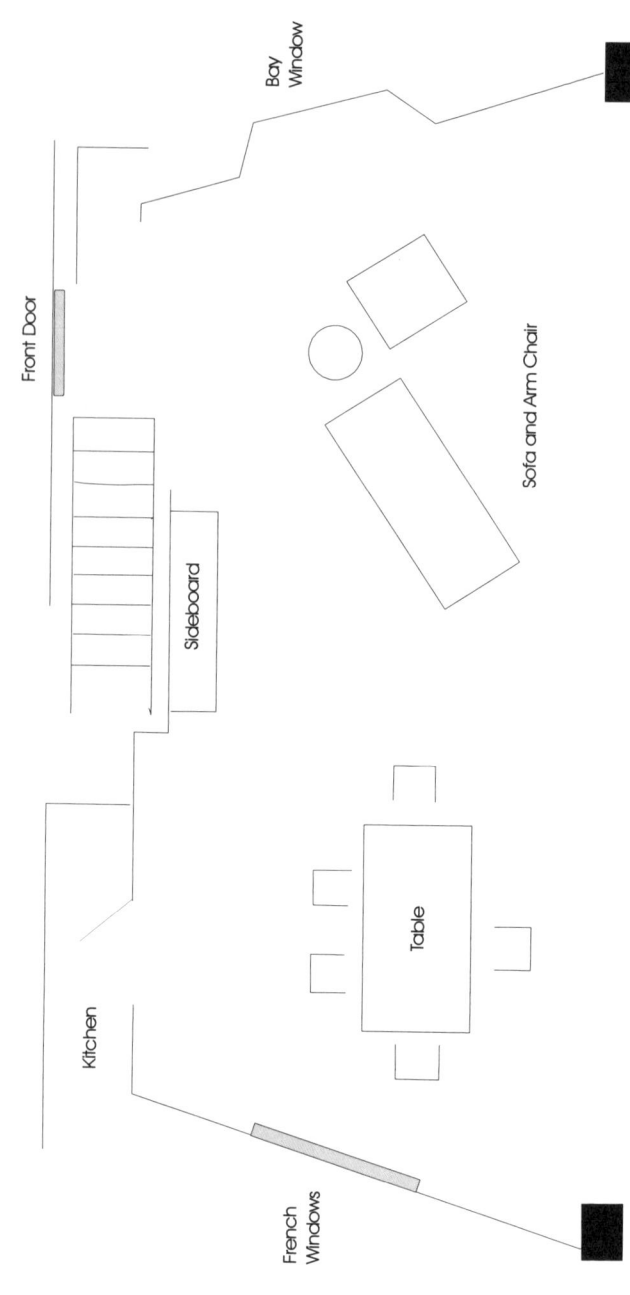